MW00680263

GROWING CREATIVE KIDS

DR. WESLEY SHARPE

BROADMAN PRESS
NASHVILLE, TENNESSEE

4260-57
ISBN: 0-8054-6057-8

Dewey Decimal Classification: 649
Subject Heading: PARENTING // CREATIVE ABILITY
Library of Congress Card Catalog Number: 92-12938
Printed in the United States of America

Scripture quotations marked RSV are from the *Revised Standard Version of the Bible,* copyrighted 1946, 1952, © 1971, 1973. Scripture quotations marked NIV are from the Holy Bible, *New International Version,* copyright © 1973, 1978, 1984 by International Bible Society.

Library of Congress Cataloging-in-Publication Data

Sharpe, Wesley, 1928-
  Growing creative kids / Wesley Sharpe
    p.   cm.
  ISBN: 0-8054-6057-8
  1. Creative thinking in children.   2. Child rearing—Religious aspects—
Christianity.   I. Title.
BF723.C5S45   1993
649′.1—dc20   92-12938
                                                                          CIP

Preface

I wish I had known more about creative thinking when my children were growing up. Accepting some of my kids' weird behavior would have been easier. Also, I think I would have spent more time laughing at their jokes, worried less about their academic grades, and held a higher view of their ideas and opinions.

My wife and I did, however, recognize God's plan for our kids, and we knew that each child was special in His sight. Created in His image. And in some way this allowed us to let their creativity burst forth.

My interest in creativity springs from a University of the Pacific graduate class I attended on "Creative Teaching." Before I began my study I believed the myth that only a few exceptionally bright and gifted children are creative. During the few months I attended the class I learned that all children are creative, not just the bright ones.

Armed with the awareness that creativity is an inborn gift, I studied the creative thinking skills of elementary school educationally handicapped children. In eight weeks of instruction these boys and girls made outstanding progress in their ability to think of more ideas, and more *original* ideas, than children without special training. From that research, the idea of *Growing Creative Kids* was born.

Like many creative ventures, several years passed before this idea evolved into a book that focused on helping parents understand and teach their children creative thinking skills. This isn't a new idea; other authors have written books for parents on how to help their children become more creative. But I believe this book's family activities, creative workouts, and suggestions for a creative development program go a step further.

Here are some things you will learn from reading *Growing Creative Kids*.

- What creative thinking is and what it isn't. And how to recognize your child's creativity.
- How creative thinking works. Where creative ideas come from, and the part imagination plays in those ideas?
- Methods parents can use to teach their preschool through elementary grade children creative thinking skills.

As a final note, I want to thank my wife Yola for her encouragement in this project. She never asked me to forget it or to try something easier. She knows the value of creativity and for twenty-five years taught her first-grade girls and boys how to be creative.

CONTENTS

PART I:

How Creativity Works

1

The Creative Promise

Creativity is a joy-filled gift that even today's busy parents can encourage in their children. Children come into the world gifted with curiosity and creative promise. Each day they look to us for help to expand their wonder-filled view of the universe. Their lively curiosity leads them in many directions as they investigate, test, and confirm their ideas, guesses, and hunches.

A few years ago I learned a little about my sons' curiosity while we fished on a small pier jutting out from the Pacific coastline. The fish, if there were any, weren't finding our offer of frozen sardines appetizing, and the boys switched to more interesting pastimes. As I watched them saw off a dead sardine's head, dissect the fish, and inspect its innards, I wondered what kind of kids I was raising.

I can't report that their curiosity led to a career in biology, or that they became skilled surgeons. I can report, however, that my sons' curiosity is apparent in the way they search Scripture for God's truth.

A Creative Model

Children's inquisitiveness shouldn't surprise parents. God, the Creator of the universe, lovingly formed us in His image (Gen. 1:26). Through His creation God has placed in each child special talents, including the ability to think creatively.

The psalmist tells parents in Psalm 127:3 that their children are God's gift and a special reward. Parents learn more about the unique nature of their children in Psalm 139:13-15.

> For thou didst form my inward parts,
> thou didst knit me together in my
>   mother's womb. . . .
> Thou knowest me right well;
> my frame was not hidden from thee,
> when I was being made in secret,
> intricately wrought in the depths of
>   the earth (RSV).

Sue Monk Kidd, a Christian writer and speaker, believes that Jesus was a model of creativity. She says that if we study Christ's life we will see His fresh and radically different personality. For example, how could the law experts and scholars of His day forsee:

- The surprise ending to Lazarus's funeral?
- Jesus surrounding Himself with little children and sticking up for their rights?
- The Master sharing a meal with prostitutes and crooked tax collectors?
- Jesus riding a donkey into Jerusalem?[1]

His example teaches us to break out of the mold and to risk new thinking. But is this goal possible for parents who want their children to think creatively?

It's no secret that raising children is incredibly hard. The countless manuals in bookstores and libraries prove that parenting is still a dark continent. Doing chores, checking homework, refereeing arguments, and ferrying children to activities are time-consuming and exhausting tasks.

For some parents helping their kids become more creative is a nightmare. How can you train a child to be a creative thinker when his favorite response is "I don't know"?

Bill Cosby tells the story of a father who entered his son's room and saw that the boy had shaved his head.

"What happened to your head?" The father asked his bald son. "Did you get a haircut?"

"I don't know," the boy replied.

"You don't know if you got a haircut? Well, tell me this: Was your head with you all day?"

"I don't know," said the boy.[2]

I suspect that this parent thinks talk about creativity is absurd. Nevertheless, creative thinking is a practical skill that parents can teach their children. The danger is that, without guidance in the use of their creative abilities, many children are afraid to take risks, and they stumble into mental ruts. Yet experts say that this does not have to happen.

Children Solve Problems

Edward De Bono is a world authority on developing children's creative thinking skills. School children in Venezuela, Japan, England, and the United States practice his methods. In fact, Venezuelan authorities thought so highly of De Bono's method of teaching creative thinking that they trained 100,000 teachers and set about teaching thinking skills to all schoolchildren. In Japan alone, 400,000 copies of his book *New Think: The Use of Lateral Thinking in the Generation of New Ideas* were sold.

De Bono believes that anyone can be taught to be creative, and a person is never too old to improve creative skills. Young children have an awe-inspiring ability to think, and they enjoy using their minds as much as they enjoy running, throwing, or jumping on a trampoline.

De Bono's book *Children Solve Problems* illustrates the creative thinking of children who were turned loose with drawing materials and instructions to draw solutions to several problems. Three of these problems were:

- How do you stop a cat and dog from fighting?
- How do you weigh an elephant?
- How do you design a fun machine?

Another of his methods is a simple technique that results in a torrent of ideas. Here's how the PMI (Plus, Minus, Interesting) works:[3]

1. Divide a sheet of paper into three columns.

2. In one column list all the positive or "plus" views of the idea. In the second column list anything that is negative or "minus" about the idea, and in the third column list the "interesting" aspects of the idea.

3. Talk over the plus, minus, and interesting parts of each PMI idea.

A *Reader's Digest* article by Edwin and Sally Kiester makes clear the value of the PMI in creative problem solving. Their article describes De Bono at work with a class of ten-year-olds. First, he asked the kids if they would like five dollars a week for going to school? An enthusiastic yes was the response. Then De Bono guided them into a PMI. "After three or four minutes of listing pluses, minuses and interesting points about the proposal, 29 out of 30 had changed their minds." Some of the minuses were:

- Parents would cut off their allowances.
- The school would raise lunch prices.

The PMI had helped these school children see that "the obvious answer wasn't necessarily the best."[4]

Using the PMI would have helped Amy, a fifth-grader, come up with creative solutions for the rejection she felt. She wrote a story that describes how children struggle when they are rebuffed by their friends.

"Once upon a time in a far-off land there was a magic farm that no one visited.

"Many different animals lived there. The odd thing about these animals was that they were different colors. The cows were pink, the horses were purple, and the hens and chicks were blue! All the pigs were green. That is except for one little fellow who was just plain pink. Nobody wanted to be near him or play with him because he wasn't green. And this little pig was very, very sad."[5]

Feelings like Amy's overwhelm some children. They want to be like their peers, and experts say too much pressure to conform can cause children to become less creative. Using creative thinking skills helps to relieve tensions and find innovative solutions to many kinds of problems. By learning to use the PMI and other creative thinking methods, potentially explosive situations are defused.

This kind of creative thinking is essential to the Christian family. Children who learn to solve problems creatively in the Christian home are better prepared to face problems in a secular environment. Creative thinking skills can be applied to the problems of daily living or the moral dilemmas that children face.

Creative and Not-So-Creative Kids

How is a child who has learned to think creatively different from one who is less creative? For one thing creative children are full of surprises. The creative child's personality characteristics are different than less creative children. They think at a different level than their peers, and they enjoy exchanging ideas. But their behavior can be frustrating, too.

Creative children who think independently and refuse to conform sometimes make parenting an unpleasant, difficult task. By comparing what is known about the behavior and personalities of highly creative children with those who are less creative, you can begin to evaluate your child's level of creativity.

The following checklist may be used to identify strengths and weaknesses in your child's creative development. The checklist can help you compare your child's creative abilities with traits important to creativity. Low creativity does not mean that your child can't become more creative. Remember, creative behavior *can* be improved.

Checklist for Identifying Creative Children

Trait	Creative Child	My Child	
		Yes	No
1. Concentration	Stays on task	___	___
2. Inquisitiveness	Burns with curiosity	___	___
3. Solves problems	Enjoys complex ideas	___	___
4. Inventiveness	Plays with ideas	___	___
5. Adaptability	Adjusts easily	___	___
6. Broad knowledge	Has many interests	___	___
7. Flexibility	Sees the other side	___	___
8. Enthusiasm	A high energy level	___	___
9. Sense of humor	Makes up jokes	___	___
10. Independence	Is self-reliant	___	___
11. Imagination	Is a daydreamer	___	___
12. Nonconforming	Sticks to his beliefs	___	___
13. Playfulness	Enjoys all play	___	___
14. Self-confident	Believes in himself	___	___

This is a good place to sound a warning about using checklists to identify creativity. Checklists are helpful as a beginning point for identifying creative behavior in children. They help you, as parents, understand some of the basic characteristics of creativity. From that point on, parents can begin to determine the extent of their child's creative abilities by observing their play and interests.

Creative Characteristics of Young Children

Very young children are creative, and experts say that preschoolers' creativity is shown in the kind of play they select and the way they express their creativity through play. During the 1986-87 school year, researchers at Ohio State University studied the creativity of four-year-old children in a preschool program. Before the special program began, four children out of a class of twenty-four were identified as highly original (creative). These four kids shared many of the same creative thinking characteristics. For example, each child was judged independent, persistent, fluent thinking, and original. There also were differences. The following is information gathered about each of these children during the year-long study.[6]

1. Shirley: According to the researchers, it was harder to pin down Shirley's creative outlet than the remaining three children. Her mom described Shirley as always busy and a kid who never said, "I don't know what to do." She expressed a multitude of ideas, and she spent long periods of time working on her pet projects.

Here is an example of her thinking. The children in her preschool class were asked, "Why do our hands have lines in them?" Most of her classmates answered, "I don't know" or "That's the way it is." Shirley's answer was more original and thoughtful. She said, "To make it easier for our hands to move."

2. Jack: Independent, strong-willed, and aggressive are adjectives that describe Jack. He also was the most academically inclined child of the group. At an early age he learned to spell his name on the family computer, count to 140, and put letters in alphabetical order.

Jack displayed two dominant creative characteristics. First, he was persistent. He spent extended periods of time building elaborate block structures and using them for his imaginative play. His second characteristic was flexible thinking. "He transformed different sized blocks into lasers, rifles, and walkie-talkies during play. He also instantaneously changed the wall of a castle into an organ keyboard, then pretended to play a few tunes. During such play, his peers would follow his lead in transforming common objects into needed props, but he originated the mental transformation."[7]

3. Audrey: Elaborate drawings, paintings, and craft work depict Audrey's creativity. If she made a mistake on a picture, she would fix it rather than start over. Audrey loved to use detail to emphasize her drawings of landscapes, animals, and people. She experimented with

marker pens, and she used different size brushes for various effects on a single painting.

"One day she painted a large heart seated on a rocking chair. When asked about this drawing, she explained that the heart represented her and her sister having a nice time in their favorite chair."[8]

4. Gary: Perhaps it was Gary's bent for storytelling that caused everyone in the preschool class to like him. Gary was a storyteller who liked elaborate detail. He also loved to pretend, and he used imaginary play and imaginary friends in his play. His favorite school play area was the housekeeping center, and that's where his creativity burst forth in dramatic play and role playing. Depending on the day, he was a doctor, dog, baby, or ghost.

He was a flexible thinker, refusing to role play the same character over and over. He also used the props in different ways. For example, if he was pretending to rush to work, or to the hospital, a briefcase became a doctor's bag or a suitcase. Finally, Gary was curious. He asked all kinds of "why" questions. He wanted a clear explanation for experiments or for what was happening in the classroom.

Creativity Starts with an Idea

Researchers have worked diligently to define creativity. Because there is disagreement about what is creative, defining creative thinking and creative problem solving isn't easy. We tend to think of creativity only as a novel invention or work of art.

No doubt these are creative products. But children who use their experience to develop new ideas, even silly ones, are beginning to think creatively. Playing around with ideas and making chance observations sometimes result in a creative work. Parents may miss the significance of creative ideas if they are too quick to silence their child. By trying to support even unusual ideas, we are encouraging creativity.

Creative ideas that we take for granted now probably

seemed silly at first. Can you imagine what people thought when they heard about:

- The astronomer Edmund Halley sitting under sixty feet of water for an hour-and-a-half testing a diving bell?
- The inventor of the parachute jumping from a balloon at 3,000 feet?
- A Scottish veterinarian named Dunlop taking time from his practice to invent a pneumatic tire?
- A radio death-ray that was supposed to shoot down airplanes but led to the development of radar?

Creative ideas and their results don't just happen. Children who are less creative must learn new ways of thinking. This is accomplished by showing them ways to increase the number and quality of their ideas. Give them freedom to express clever, foolish, or whimsical ideas without being criticized or judged.

Researchers who want to stimulate creative thinking tell children to express their ideas as rapidly as possible. In one study 375 children were asked to think of ideas for improving a toy fire truck. Some of the children were trained by using questions that would help to stimulate their thinking. The children who received the training produced more ideas. Also, their ideas were more flexible and clever than the children with no training.[9]

Creative problem solving can be applied to a variety of situations including relationships, moral questions, and appropriate behavior. Experience with creative children shows they often are rebellious youngsters. They operate relatively free of conventional restraints and with their own set of values and ethical standards. This may be why creative children, even when under strong pressure to conform, tend to remain independent. Creative problem solving eases the stress and tension parents feel because it provides a system geared to accept and evaluate ideas in an open and friendly atmosphere.

Points to Remember

1. The true source of beauty and creativity is God, and we are shaped in His image. Your child's creativity is a gift from God. Encourage it.

2. Part of being a parent is keeping a child's curiosity alive by supplying the materials and activities.

3. Parents encourage curiosity by their example. In other words, be curious, too.

4. Children think creatively when they use their ability and experience to produce something new to them.

5. It is OK to get excited and express ideas that seem silly.

6. If your child's ideas are unacceptable, discuss and evaluate them together.

Family Activities

The following activities encourage curiosity and the smooth flow of ideas. Allowing ideas to flow is a skill that children can learn and use to solve many different types of problems.

1. *Practice a PMI.*—Get the kids together and choose a problem that is troubling your family. Ask each member for ideas to solve the problem. When at least five ideas have been given use the following form to test the ideas. For example, write down idea one. List the plus, minus, and interesting aspects of it. Then go to the second and third ideas. When the PMI is completed choose the solutions that are best for your family.

Problem: (State in one sentence)._____

	Plus	*Minus*	*Interesting*
Ideas			
1.			
2.			

2. *Play an imagination game.*—Imagination games are activities that are fun and that can be played by the family. The following game should be read by a family member while the others participate. During the game ask each person to:

    a. Imagine or pretend you are doing what you are asked to do.

    b. Answer the questions silently.

    c. Close your eyes, get comfortable, and relax.

The name of the game is "The Bird Cage."

Ready? Eyes closed? Comfortable? Pretend that you have a bird cage.

Did you see it? . . . What colors do you see? . . . How big is the bird cage?

Put a bird inside the cage. . . . Make it whatever kind of bird you want it to be. . . . Change the bird's color. . . . Is it the same bird? Make the bird bigger. . . . How big is the bird now? . . . Will it fit in the cage?

Now make the bird into the largest one you can imagine. What does it look like? . . . What happened to the cage?

Give the bird a name. Ask the bird to come to you. . . . Climb on its back and ask for a ride. . . . Be sure to give it directions. . . . Fly anywhere you want to go. . . . Where did you go? . . . Was it fun?

Now fly back into the cage. How did it feel to fly? . . . Make the bird small again. . . . Say good-bye. Let the bird and cage disappear.

Draw a picture of the bird and its cage. Place the name of the bird at the bottom of the picture.

Checklist of fourteen ways to encourage your child's curiosity.

Preschool

    1. Kids' questions signal a genuine interest. Take time to listen. If the question is jumbled, decide what she is trying to ask.

2. "Why?" questions deserve an answer. Don't give up when they come one after the other, but try to answer all your child's questions.
3. Keep your answers appropriate for your child's age level. You will lose him with a long explanation if a few words will do it.
4. When you are answering questions use concrete examples, pictures, or simple experiments.

Early Elementary

1. Make a list of your child's questions and check them off as they are answered.
2. Keep a wide range of books handy for answering questions. When your child is curious about a topic help her find the information.
3. Use simple experiments to illustrate a point. For example, plant vegetable seeds and help your child keep track of the growth cycle.
4. Buy toys that use gravity, show how gears work, or illustrate a mechanical principle.
5. Pay attention to your child's interests. Does he like music, math, or sports? Try to give him opportunities to develop these skills.

Late Elementary

These are the grades where many children become less creative.

1. If you are working on a project, explain what you are doing and why you became interested in it.
2. List the ways you can keep your child's curiosity alive. Then do something about it.
3. Teach beginning research skills. Does your child know how to find information? Show him how to use the library's card catalog or its computerized information system.
4. Reading stimulates and satisfies curiosity. Is your child reading a variety of materials? Check her reading interests.

5. Find games that will inspire your child's questions and aid in his search for answers.

Notes

1. Sue Monk Kidd, "Living on the Creative Edge," *Signs of the Times,* January 1991.

2. Bill Cosby, *Fatherhood* (New York: Doubleday, 1986), 18.

3. "Interview Edward De Bono." *Omni,* March 1988.

4. Edwin and Sally Kiester, "How to Teach Your Child to Think," *Reader's Digest,* June 1991, 142.

5. E. Paul Torrance, *Rewarding Creative Behavior* (Englewood Cliffs: Prentice-Hall, 1965), 240.

6. Lynn G. Johnson and E. J. Amos, "A Descriptive Study of the Creative and Social Behavior of Four Highly Original and Young Children," *The Journal of Creative Behavior,* 24 (1990): 216.

7. Ibid., 209.

8. Ibid., 216.

9. E. Paul Torrance, *Education and the Creative Potential* (Minneapolis: The University of Minnesota, 1964).

2

Imagination:
The Creative Spark Plug

A favorite book of my children was a worn-out, dog-eared volume of Bible stories. Even when family devotions ended in giggles, the kids listened attentively when I read one of the stories. They never seemed to grow tired of them, and we read some stories over and over.

There is a reason why the Old and New Testament stories captivate children. A good story is one they can touch and feel with their imaginations. When children travel on imaginary flights, they use the mysterious and artistic side of the brain where feelings, emotions, dreams, and creativity are born.

God created us with a brain that functions in logical, emotional, and creative ways. The logical side of the brain is in control when children learn story facts. But when they go beyond factual information, they are beginning to think creatively.

Children's Use of Imagination

Bible stories like Jonah's (Jonah 1—4) touch the creative imagination of children, and the creative part of their brain is in command when they:

- Picture the storm and the sea spray driving across the bow of the tiny ship.
- Feel the fear of the ship's crew before Jonah is hurled overboard.
- Imagine Jonah sitting in the great fish's belly with the water sloshing around him.

I have a simple assignment for you. Read the story of Samson and Delilah to your child (Judg. 16:1-31). Before you begin, ask your child to imagine that he was a neighbor of Samson or Delilah. Ask him to draw a mental picture of the way Israel looked when Samson lived there. After you have read the story ask your child to complete the following sentences:

1. Samson was _____ .

2. Delilah felt _____ .

3. If I was Samson's neighbor _____ .

4. When the temple fell _____ .

5. The god Dagon looked _____ .

6. God was_____ .

7. I lived near the temple and_____ .

Are your child's answers more factual or imaginative? If the answers go beyond the facts of the story, your child's thinking has shifted to the creative, imaginative side of the brain.

Logical and Imaginative Thinking

To be able to think imaginatively and to accomplish balanced thinking, the brain is divided into left and right hemispheres. Our thinking shifts from left to right depending on the task. Unlike the brains of animals, each hemisphere of the human brain specializes in highly complex methods of thinking. This is possible because a thick nerve cable with millions of fibers connects the two hemispheres, allowing us to shift back and forth between the two halves.

The two halves of the brain have different but overlapping ways of thinking:

Left		Right	
Positive	Verbal	Intuitive	Nonverbal
Analytical	Concrete	Spontaneous	Visual
Linear	Rational	Holistic	Playful
Explicit	Active	Diffuse	Symbolic
Sequential	Goal oriented	Artistic	Physical

Most of us tap the left brain when we are using language, but the right hemisphere is in charge when we are in touch with our feelings. Left-handers appear to be an exception. While about 98 percent of the right-handed people are left-brain dominant, only two thirds of the lefties have dominant left brains. What about the other one third who are left-handed? It may be that the right hemisphere dominates the verbal role of their brains, and the left brain controls emotions.

Does it make a difference if we are left-brain dominant or right-brain dominant? Balance is the important ingredient. Imagine how unpleasant it is to be around someone whose right brain completely dominates his feelings and emotions. On the other hand, a left-brain dominant thinker, whose literal thinking lacks emotion, is not the kind of person most of us enjoy.

The ability to shift between the hemispheres is what's important. The professional artist uses the right brain for creative work, but to keep accurate accounts, she must call on the left brain. And a chemist works in a left brain occupation, but when he is having fun away from the job, he is using his right brain.

Left- or Right-Brain Thinking?

Priscilla Donovan and Jacquelyn Wonder in their book *Whole Brain Thinking* describe how the left and right sides of the brain respond to different kinds of humor.

The two sides of the brain react or understand humor in two different ways, and to appreciate a joke fully both sides must be in use. The left is quite literal in its interpretations of the joke and is especially drawn to word play. The right is more alert to the subtleties and nuances.[1]

A left-brain thinker would chuckle at the joke: "The bigger the summer vacation the harder the fall." But the same person would puzzle over the story of a young man who returned from a blind date with Siamese twins. His friend inquired, "Did you have a good time?" He replied, "yes and no."

From all appearances we are a left-brained culture, substituting rote learning and literal thinking for creativity. In many instances we aren't using our right brains or encouraging our children to shift from left- to right-brain thinking. Parents and teachers often reward left-brain thinking at the expense of the creative right-side thinking. Marilee Zendek notes,

> The left-brain dominant schoolgirl who remembers names, adds numbers properly, and works with a great sense of order and tidiness is praised and gets a star beside her name. The right-brain dominant child who daydreams and stares at distant clouds preferring to make up stories rather than learn her lesson is sent home with a disciplinary note.[2]

Children can learn to develop the skills of the less-preferred side. Many children can make the shift from left- to right-brain thinking. Others become stuck in one hemisphere or the other and end up using the wrong side of the brain for the thinking they need to do.

Find Your Child's Preference

If you're not sure whether your child is left- or right-brain dominant, the following quiz may help you get a picture of which side he prefers. Preferences are developed early, and as children find success with one side, it becomes more dominant. The child who is better at art than reading will develop a preference for art and neglect reading. When this happens the chance of abilities becoming more one-sided increases.

These statements describe left- and right-brain qualities. Try to decide which ones best describe your child.

1. Teacher's comments:
   a. He's a dreamer. Lives in another world.
   b. Focuses on tasks. The first to finish and is always right.
2. Completing homework:
   a. Plans assignments and turns them in on time.
   b. Can lose an assignment between her desk and the teacher's desk.
3. Understanding math:
   a. Likes to think logically and figure out problems.
   b. Math is OK, but prefers other subjects.
4. Verbal Communication:
   a. Never stops talking.
   b. A better listener than speaker.
5. Expressing feelings:
   a. Moans and groans—has mood swings.
   b. Controls his emotions. Grits his teeth and does it.
6. Completing jobs at home:
   a. Follows a checklist and likes routine.
   b. Lets it happen. Jobs are completed but sloppy.
7. Paying attention to schedules:
   a. Means well but forgets what to do.
   b. Always prompt.
8. Playing games:
   a. A whiz at Pictionary.
   b. Unbeatable at Scrabble.
9. Playing sports:
   a. Competitive, happy when winning.
   b. Plays for the fun of it.

10. Enjoying humor:
    a. Appreciates the subtleties in jokes.
    b. Favorite jokes play on words.
11. Responding to discipline:
    a. Follows the rules.
    b. Seems to feel rules are made to be broken.

Scoring: Items 1b, 2a, 3a, 4a, 5b, 6a, 7b, 8b, 9a, 10b, and 11a are left-dominant characteristics.

Self-Esteem and Creativity

We know children can develop the less-preferred side of the brain and become more balanced creative thinkers, but there are blocks to creative thinking. In many instances a major block to right-brain thinking and creativity is emotional stress. Long-standing anxiety or depression nearly always stands in the way of freewheeling, creative thinking.

Children may cover up their anxiety and learn to put on a good front, but anxiety cripples creative thinking. Deep emotional stress restricts their ability to shift to the creative side of the brain. These children feel safe in an undemanding routine that lowers their anxiety but fails to inspire creativity.

Sometimes the important relationship between creativity and emotional health isn't recognized. Nevertheless, the more children become tangled in a web of problems, the greater the likelihood that right-brain skills will stop developing. To get back on track the child requires psychologically safe surroundings where creativity can blossom.

Psychologist Abraham Maslow, speaking about children's creativity, was on target when he said, "It is terribly impressive that the relationship with psychiatric health or psychological health is crucial, so profound, so terribly important, and so obvious, and yet it is not used as a foundation on which to build."[3]

The child's self-esteem is the bridge between good mental health and creative thinking. Children who feel good about themselves have a greater chance of being productive, creative thinkers than children who feel worthless and unlovable. This means that children with low self-esteem can make only weak attempts at being creative.[4]

Some children misjudge the truth about themselves. They appear to be well-adjusted, but if you talk to them, their attitude oozes defeat. They can't believe they are good, smart, handsome, pretty, or worthy of praise.

Here is a sample of common feelings children with low self-esteem experience. In one way or another they say:

- I'm bad.
- I can't be trusted.
- Kids don't like me.
- My parents aren't happy with me.

Contrast those feelings with the feelings of high self-esteem children. Children who think positively about themselves say:

- I'm good.
- My parent's approve of me.
- I do what I say I'll do.
- Kids like me.
- My parents love me.

When Self-Esteem Nose-dives

As parents, you have an enormous effect on your child's self-esteem. Parents and other significant people in a child's life help form self-esteem. You may love, accept, and approve of your child. Unless, however, these feelings filter through to your youngster, she will not believe she measures up to your standards. When this happens self-esteem zooms downward.

Furthermore, the messages children get at home and at school frequently reinforce left-brain thinking and increase emotional distress. Instead of focusing on the child's inventiveness, curiosity, and humor; academic success and good behavior are stressed. Children soon learn to knuckle under, and it only takes a few unhappy experiences before they understand that creativity is rated lower than conformity. Horror stories are not hard to find. For example:

> Tim stomped into the kitchen and banged his backpack on the table. "Can you believe it?" he yelled at his surprised mother.
>
> Without waiting for a reply he jabbed his finger at his poem. Written in red ink and heavily underlined was his teacher's comment. "F . . . This is wrong. Next time follow directions."

The assignment given Tim was "Give three reasons why spring is your favorite season." He hadn't intentionally disobeyed, but his creative fantasy led him in another direction, and he wrote a poem telling why he loved summer.

It's not only in school that children learn to suppress their creativity. Some parents fail to understand how important what they think and say is to their children.

> Judy, a ten-year-old fourth-grader, proudly handed her mother a story she had written at school. After reading it, her mother angrily threw the paper into the waste basket. Judy had written a story with dirty words in it. It didn't matter that it was a playful, humorous, and creative story. The result was that she felt ashamed and worthless, and her mother felt frustrated and alienated.

Certainly Tim and Judy will think twice before they stray too far into creative right-brain thinking. In both cases the parents failed to encourage their child's creativity.

Perhaps children like Judy and Tim will feel less pressure to conform if their parents:

- Discuss the unacceptable parts of the poem or story. These children may not understand why their writing is unsatisfactory. Listen to your child's side of the story before you act.

- Help rewrite the material. Judy and Tim's parents will encourage their children's creative thinking if they work with them on their assignments.
- Encourage them to continue writing. Tim and Judy were disheartened by failure, and their parent's encouragement will nudge them forward.
- Ask them to write something for the family. Writing a special story or poem will boost their self-esteem and creative thinking.
- Praise their originality and creativity. There's a chance Judy and Tim will continue to write if they are rewarded for trying.
- Talk to the teacher about the problem. The next step for Tim's mother is a conference. So far the only story she has heard is Tim's.
- Control their anger. Yelling at the child or teacher about the problem poem or story will not help either of these kids.

Plan for Creative Growth

Regardless of what happens at school, parents can provide an atmosphere that encourages originality and imaginative thinking. There is little chance of creative growth unless a plan is set in motion to encourage resourcefulness, inventiveness, and unusual ideas. Here are a few suggestions:

1. Start a fantasy-land corner. Display a poem, story, drawing, or creative thought for the day.
2. Encourage younger children to invent a tall tale. Use a tape recorder and replay the story.
3. Start telling a story and ask your child for input. Ask for different story endings, and let your child choose the best.
4. If a child has reading or academic problems, find out

what right-side activity he enjoys. Talk about riddles, jokes, and dreams.

There is hope for children who seem to have lost the gift for zany, playful creativity. In Scripture we learn that the Spirit of God is the Spirit of creativity. Parents are assured that their children have received God's gift of creativity. As children learn to open their lives to Him, their potential for creativity grows.

Points to Remember

1. Learning to use both sides of the brain is the secret for developing creativity. The goal is balanced thinking between the brain's left and right hemispheres.

2. Laugh with your children. Laugh at the funny things they do and the funny things they write.

3. The child who feels emotions strongly and expresses them clearly is using both sides of the brain.

4. Most school programs emphasize left-brain skills. Parents can balance this out by encouraging right-brain values.

5. Emotional stress slows down the child's ability to shift into the creative thinking mode.

6. Children who are emotionally stressed require a psychological refuge where they can stargaze, reflect, and wonder about things.

7. Be understanding and empathetic. Work toward developing your child's personality.

Family Activities

The goal of these activities is to develop integrated whole-brain thinking and improve creativity. Try to observe your child's shifts from left to right-brain thinking. Find ways to encourage the use of the right brain and to recognize the activities which cause shifts from one hemisphere to the other. For instance:

1. Read a Bible story and ask your child some factual

questions. Next, read the passage a second time, but instead of facts discuss the meaning of the passage. Finally, ask your child to pretend he is a character in the story and dramatize it.

2. Set up a bulletin board and invent a private language of words and pictures. Use it to leave special messages on the bulletin board.

3. Teach younger children more than just the name of an object. Help them to learn that the label is only a small part of the whole. For example, if your child is learning about a tree include touching and smelling it. Help her to imagine the inside of the tree, and the parts that grow underground. How do birds, moths, and bugs use the tree? Ask "In what part of the tree would you like to live?"

Checklist for Building Self-Esteem

1. Communicate your love. Don't hold back; show and tell your love. Children who know they are loved can tackle problems head on.

2. Have a reasonable discipline policy allowing you to ease up or set limits. Learn when to let go and laugh and when to be firm. Before acting decide if disciplinary action is truly necessary.

3. Accept the positive and negative feelings of your children. For instance, don't expect an angry child to be filled with love for you.

4. Be a realistic role model. Let your child see how you cope with frustrations and disappointments. Kids learn by example. If you throw a temper tantrum expect to see the same behavior from your child.

5. Encourage independent thinking. Set reasonable expectations and be an active, sympathetic listener.

6. Teach your child to know and accept limitations. Remember to be tolerant of mistakes. By taking the stigma out of failure, you can discourage your child's efforts to be perfect.

7. Provide time for your kid to pursue his or her talents

and interests without interference. Point out that life is a series of opportunities.

Notes

1. Jacquelyn Wonder and Priscilla Donovan, *Whole Brain Thinking* (New York: William Morrow, 1984), 106.

2. Marilee Zendek, *The Right Brain Experience* (New York: McGraw Hill, 1983), 12.

3. C. W. Taylor, ed., *Creativity and Progress* (New York: McGraw-Hill, 1964), 368.

4. Cecelia Yau, "An Essential Interrelationship: Healthy Self-Esteem and Productive Creativity," *The Journal of Creative Behavior* 25 (1991).

3

Creative Kids: Not Cookie-Cutter Kids

Mattie Pearl Simmons was an excellent judge of musical talent, but several years passed before she knew the extent of her son Calvin's ability.

Mrs. Simmons directed the gospel choir at San Francisco's Mt. Zion Baptist Church. One Sunday morning while leading the choir, she turned around and saw three-year-old Calvin waving his arms, too. At the age of six, when most children learn to read, he was reading music. A year later Mattie Pearl hired a music teacher for Calvin because he had gone beyond what she could teach him.

Mattie Pearl Simmons was a parent who nurtured her child's creativity. She believed that what she did as a parent mattered, and she was unwilling to sit back and do nothing. Because she understood that Calvin required special care to develop his creative ability, she was determined to help his musical talent blossom. What she didn't know was that Calvin eventually would direct the Oakland Symphony.[1]

Parenting Styles Make a Difference

Unfortunately, there are parents who fail to see the damaging effects of their parenting style on their child's creative ability. Here are some facts about parenting practices that have a negative influence on the creative thinking of children.

1. Children who lack discipline are less creative than children who have constraints placed on their behavior.

Susan is an example of a child whose parents did not understand the value of discipline.

Over coffee with friends, Susan's mother said, "Susan is creative enough to make her own decisions, and we let her do what she wants to do." While her mother talked, Susan rudely interrupted her and chatted incessantly. Smiling, her mother tried to ignore her, but Susan refused to be overlooked. She whined and tugged at her mother until her mom whisked her from the room.

Afraid that discipline would destroy her creativity, Susan's parents relaxed their authority and let her have her way. The sad part is that they weren't nurturing her creative ability, and their lack of discipline was hurting her creative development. Total freedom is destructive to creative thinking, and children like Susan end up frustrated and unhappy when they finally must face up to their behavior.

2. Parents who are overbearing and demand obedience and conformity from their children tip the scales away from creativity. Heavy-handed discipline is just as harmful to a child's creative development as no discipline.

Researchers have probed the effects of authoritarian and nonauthoritarian parents on children's creativity. A study was made of young men and women who were National Merit Finalists. Those who thought their parents were authoritarian were compared with those who judged their parents to be nonauthoritarian. The results show that children are less original and creative if their parents insist on unquestioned obedience.[2]

3. A rigid academic program does not develop creativity. Creative thinking is dulled by instruction that leads to overreliance on established ways of thinking. Parents sometimes are fooled by the high grades and good teachers' reports. Grades and reports may be poor indicators of creative ability.

On the other hand, the ability to dream up unusual ideas is linked to creative thinking. When parents promote and accept their children's fresh, inventive ideas, they are advancing creative thinking.

Surprising Ideas

The Invention Convention is an excellent illustration of how kids can think of fresh, inventive ideas if they are given the opportunity. Every year each child in this third grade class at Camino Pablo Elementary School in Moraga, California, is required to invent something original, and the kids come up with some beauties.

A recent crop of inventions included a water-saving device that shuts off the shower, ready or not; a battery-run back scratcher for pets; and a basketball launcher for little kids whose shots fall short of the basket.

One boy invented an elaborate security system to keep roaming dogs and cats off his front lawn. It used motion sensors and automatic timers to set off sprinklers, plus a taped recording of a roaring lion. The only problem was his system couldn't tell the difference between a wandering dog and the church's pastor.[3]

Children's ideas don't have to be in the form of an invention to be creative because much of what they say is creative, too. After a hard day, parents often tune out what children say, but they may miss some surprisingly creative ideas.

The following statements by five to nine-year-old children are examples of children's verbal creative thinking.

- Lloyd, age seven, said on a foggy day, "If the church steeple didn't hold the fog up like a tent pole, it would all fall down and smother us."
- Marcia, age eight, said, "Love is kinda like heart trouble."
- Mark, age nine, returning from an overnight hike said, "The moon is a flashlight in the sky."
- Kevin, age five, said on a blustery day, "The wind is grouchy today."[4]

Jerome Stattler, professor at San Diego State University, believes that children become more creative when parents show respect for, and confidence in, their children. Parents have a great opportunity. Each day they can listen to their children's ideas and talk together about them. Rather than endlessly giving advice, they can give their children a chance for greater freedom to think originally.[5]

A Problem-Solving Method

Here's where brainstorming comes in. Brainstorming gives parents a chance to encourage their children to think independently and to be partners in creative problem solving. It is basic to the development of creative thinking because it inspires children to express unique ideas. When children brainstorm, their ideas aren't choked off, and the friendly atmosphere of the sessions preserves their self-esteem.

At the start brainstorming is essentially a right-brain activity, and children can pour out their ideas. This is the imaginative part of brainstorming, and the criticism of ideas is banned. Family members are free to use their intuition and to be flexible in their thinking. The left brain comes into play later during the evaluation of the ideas and the selection of the best ones.

Brainstorming works because it provides a responsive, encouraging, safe environment that is open to new ideas. In this atmosphere children learn the cues leading to creative, imaginative thinking. Brainstorming teaches youngsters to play with ideas and to produce a large number of ideas leading to the solution of a problem.

The technique has day-to-day family applications. Keeping rooms clean, settling arguments, planning vacations, and discussing the consequences of an action are problems that can be solved by brainstorming.

The basic strategy for this kind of thinking is to delay judging the merit of ideas until all of the ideas have been listed. If children's ideas are judged at the same time they are expressed, the creative thinking process becomes less effective. Prejudging restricts the flow of good ideas. When children begin to evaluate their ideas too quickly, they worry about whether the ideas are good or bad, and fewer good ideas are triggered.

To illustrate this point, find a piece of notebook paper. Think about a problem that has bothered you recently. List all of the ways you can think of to solve this problem.

1. Think only of good ideas.
2. List only good ideas.

Remember, don't jot down any ideas unless you think it is a good one. Give yourself a time limit of three or four minutes to complete your list.

Now think of another problem. List all of the ways you can think of to solve this problem.

1. Let the ideas flow.
2. Forget about whether they are good or poor ideas.
3. Don't judge the idea until you have finished your list.

To finish the experiment in idea production, count the ideas in each list. The second list should be longer and if you evaluate your ideas, they will be better ones.

Brainstorming is a basic method that develops and enhances the creative thinking of children. When children brainstorm they are looking for new ideas rather than hanging on to old ones. It is a thinking method that teaches children to express ideas and to evaluate them later. When children discover that they won't be criticized for expressing silly or crazy ideas, they feel better about themselves, and their improved self-esteem generates new confidence in their abilities.

Helping Toddlers and Preschool Children Learn Problem Solving

Children must solve problems each day. These problems range from simple ones ("What socks should I wear to school?") to serious ones ("What can I do about the boy that hates me?"). Even small children can learn to problem solve if the problems are kept at a simple level.

Here are six suggestions for teaching tiny tots problem-solving skills.

1. Don't ask yes/no questions; keep them open-ended.
2. See how many answers can be generated in a few minutes. Don't worry if the answers are outlandish or unrealistic.
3. Try for unconventional uses of ordinary things. For instance, a pillow could be a stool.
4. Try to come up with unusual responses to questions like: "I wonder what would happen if . . .
   a. Jesus came for breakfast?
   b. Jesus was my school teacher?
   c. I gave away all my toys?
   d. Nobody liked me?"
5. Make up a simple story with a problem and talk about ways to solve the problem.

Points to Remember

1. Our potential for creativity increases as we allow God's Spirit to teach and guide us.

2. Encourage your child's creative abilities by eliminating parenting practices that offer too much freedom or set impossible limits.

3. Be enthusiastic and encourage good work habits.

4. There is a difference between parents who assert their authority and parents who are authoritarian. Research has shown that children of authoritarian parents are less creative than other children.

5. Creative behavior is not enhanced by allowing children to do as they please.

6. It is easy to miss the creative expressions of children. Listen to what your child says.

7. Deferring judgment of ideas is a basic concept of brainstorming.

8. Toddlers and preschoolers can learn problem solving skills.

Family Activities

1. To capitalize on new ideas, make a chart of creative expressions. When you judge something to be creative

say: "I like what you said. I'm going to put it on a chart for the family to see."

2. Make a fun and zany family scrapbook of fabulous sayings. Add photos, cartoons, or jokes that the family enjoys.

3. Play left-brain/right brain games like Bible Pictionary.

4. Choose a problem that relates to your family. Decide on a time limit for discussion and choose a family member to record ideas and possible solutions. List the ideas without analyzing or criticizing them, then select the best solutions to the problem.

5. Make a chart of the brainstorming rules and the Discovery Checklist. Display the chart during family brainstorming meetings.

Brainstorming Rules Chart

1. Free your imagination.
2. Wait to judge the ideas.
3. The more ideas the better.
4. Combined your ideas to make them better.

Discovery Checklist[6]

Discovery Questions	What Happens?
1. Can I take part of it away?	_____
2. Can I change its color?	_____
3. Can I find another use for it?	_____
4. Can I multiply or divide it?	_____
5. Can I make it smaller or larger?	_____
6. Can I take it apart and rebuild it?	_____
7. Can I change its position?	_____
8. Can I give it light?	_____
9. Can I give it touch or odor?	_____
10. Can I give it motion or sound?	_____

Notes

1. *The Tribune*, Oakland, California, September 18, 1988, C6.

2. Jerome Sattler, *Assessment of Children* (San Diego: Jerome M. Sattler, 1988).

3. Kelly Gust, "Bright Kids," *The Tribune*, March 22, 1991.

4. James Smith, *Creative Teaching of the Language Arts in the Elementary School* (Boston: Allyn and Bacon, 1967), adapted from page 100.

5. Jerome Sattler, *Assessment of Children* (San Diego: Jerome M. Sattler, 1988), 683.

6. A. Osborn, *Applied Imagination* (New York: Charles Scribner's Sons, 1963).

PART II:

Homes that Grow Creative Kids

4

Dispelling
Myths About
Creative Thinking

How well do you understand creative thinking? Do you believe your child's creativity is a lost cause? Do you continue to think that only the sharpest kids can think imaginatively?

Let's consider a few of the myths about creativity and creative thinking. Many of the myths are hard core ones, and once parents believe them, they are difficult to discard. Also, these falsehoods are easy to accept, and, if you believe them, they will affect the way you treat your child's creative gift.

The following quiz will help you separate fact from fiction. Take a few minutes to read each statement and jot down the letter of the answer you think is correct. It isn't a scientifically developed test, but I hope you will find it is fun and teaches about creative thinking too.

Choose the best response for each statement.

1. When the teacher says Jimmy's ideas are creative she means:
   a. He knows ten ways to get out of homework.
   b. He's a tricky little rascal.
   c. He's a math genius.
   d. He thinks differently than other children.
2. Sara finishes her assignment in fifteen minutes, then wanders around the classroom. This is a sign that:
   a. She is bored.
   b. She took a speed-reading class.

45

    c. Her I.Q. is in the stratosphere.

    d. It has nothing to do with creative thinking.

3. The twins are scatterbrained and fail to follow through on their ideas. Their teacher is correct when he says:

    a. The twins are highly creative.

    b. This is typical behavior for twins.

    c. They eat too much junk food.

    d. Only ideas that result in a product are creative.

4. Jake plods along in class. He does what he's asked to do and nothing more. He won't try new games or activities. His parents believe that:

    a. Jake's creative talents will emerge.

    b. He is creative but shy.

    c. He is a prodigy waiting to be discovered.

    d. Unless he is encouraged he will lose his creative gift.

5. Emma's parents know she is creative. They are waiting for her to blossom. Her parents are:

    a. Right. Creative ideas come out of the blue.

    b. Right. That's the way Albert Einstein developed.

    c. Right. Creative people don't study.

    d. Wrong. Sometimes years of preparation precede a creative product.

6. No one in Bobby's class understands what he is talking about. That includes his teacher.

    a. His complex thinking proves he's creative.

    b. His doctor says, "Cut out the sugar."

    c. If it isn't complex it isn't creative.

    d. Often simple ideas are creative ones.

7. June's dad doesn't believe she is creative. He says, "Anything that's useful has already been invented."

    a. True. New ideas are rehashed old ones.

    b. True. Normal people aren't inventors.

    c. True. Most bosses don't like new ideas.

    d. False. Some simple ideas are big winners.

If you answered letter "d" for all the questions you were 100 percent correct, and you can distinguish between legend and truth. Now go ahead and read more about the myths.

Myths About Creative Thinking

In his book *Imagineering,* Michael LeBoeuf lists several myths about creativity. Let's see if you recognize them:[1]

Myth 1: To Be Creative Means Imagining or Doing Something New

This myth pops up regularly. Actually, there is very little creative thinking that is new and original. If you believe this myth, you may miss out on the fun of watching your child's creativity soar. Be prepared to listen to her nonstop chatter about a new math concept or her next literature assignment.

Children need to have a certain amount of background knowledge before they come up with a creative solution. But most experts define creative thinking as the way your child approaches and solves problems.

Myth 2: Only a Genius Is Creative

Some individuals with 150 IQ's are extremely creative at what they choose to do. But the opposite is also true. The high IQ person can be a rigid, noncreative thinker since intelligence test results reveal nothing about creative thinking.

Terman's study of a group of geniuses (IQ of 140 or higher) started with 1,500 children and followed them through adulthood. Although they were respected members of their communities and contributed to their professions, their creative achievements didn't match their high IQs.

Myth 3: Creativity Is Impractical and Borders on Insanity

This myth is based on the theory that you have to be a little crazy to be creative. Or if not slightly crazy, then at least impractical and scatterbrained.

The test of a creative idea is its usefulness. It is hard to imagine someone who is either insane, scatterbrained, or impractical coming up with creative solutions. Don't be fooled. If what your child is producing is useless, she isn't thinking creatively.

Creative thinking springs from good mental health. Children need the freedom to risk new ideas. Low self-esteem, anxiety, and fear are creativity killers.

Myth 4: If You Have Creative Ability, Your Talents Will Be Discovered

Without training, many children begin to lose their creative thinking skills by the fourth grade. As they grow older, their creativity is buried under rigid and conforming attitudes and thinking. Children's creativity thrives on motivation, encouragement, and praise. Without encouragement their creative talents may be hidden under a blanket of anxiety and low self-esteem.

Myth 5: Ideas Are Like Magic; You Don't Have to Work for Them

Rhonda Zwillinger, in an article written for *Psychology Today,* states: "It takes at least 10 years of immersion in a given domain before an eminent creator is likely to be able to make a distinctive mark. . . . Einstein, for example, who is popularly thought to have doodled out the theory of relativity at age 26 in his spare time, was in fact compulsively engaged in thinking about the problem at least from the age of 16."[2]

Ideas sometimes come as you relax before dropping off to sleep or at other unexpected times. These flashes aren't magic. They signal the many hours you have spent thinking about a problem and its solution.

Myth 6: Creativity Means Complexity

If this statement is true some of the essential products we use might not exist. For example, something as simple yet useful as masking tape wasn't invented until 1925.

Myth 7: The Best Way Has Already Been Found

At least one company, 3M, doesn't believe this myth. It encourages its employees to spend 15 percent of their work time thinking and developing ideas.[3]

Small ideas still count. "The adhesive bandage, safety pin, paper cup and soda can pop-top were 'small' ideas. Still, they were prime examples of imagination, curiosity, common sense and hard work."[4]

Where Creativity Prospers

If you haven't shaken these myths from your thinking, there is a chance your kids won't reach their creative potential. Furthermore, creativity vanishes when parents believe the myths and insist that their children always conform rather than be unpredictable. Psychologists Julius and Zelda Segal point out that "the childhood histories of many creative men and women reveal . . . growing up in homes where an infectious enthusiasm for creative endeavors was virtually a way of life."[5]

The point is that parents shouldn't wait until their children enter kindergarten or first grade to encourage creative thinking. A toddler's flashes of creative talent may be difficult to recognize and sometimes may be obscured by their behavior. However, the behavior that parents tend to overlook or find exasperating may actually be the first flicker of creative behavior. For example:

- The two-year-old that scribbles on a table cloth, magazine cover, phone book, or calendar may become a gifted artist.
- The child who tosses a ball with smooth as silk coordination may become a super athlete.
- The preschooler who asks you to sing his favorite songs over and over may become a creative musician.
- The kid who won't leave the family computer alone may become an inventive programmer.

Parents make a major contribution to their child's inborn creativity. There is no doubt that "In communicating our own enthusiasm for the joys of creative pursuits, we are increasing the chances of a creative life for our young."[6]

Teach Your Child Persistence

Persistence is an important trait. Like all of us, kids get discouraged and want to give up or stop when they don't find an easy solution to a problem. As the creative role model for your kids, you can show them how to be persistent by modeling persistence. Here are four useful tips to help encourage your child's persistence.[7]

1. *Overpower the impulse to do your child's work for him.*—Find some way to keep your child from depending on you. Bite your tongue if necessary, but don't give your kid the answer to a problem, choose the color for his painting, or write his story ending. It takes determined parents to walk away when their child is struggling for an answer, but it may be necessary to convince him that he can finish without your help.

2. *Allow time for creativity.*—A child's day is filled with a myriad of activities. To be creative, children need time to begin a project and see it through to the end. Kids have competing commitments, too. And you may need to help them find time in their daily schedule to work on a pet project.

3. *Be a model.*—The mom who continues to work on a frustrating sewing project sends a better message about persistence than if she gave a five-minute lecture on "finishing what you start."

4. *Be your child's advocate.*—Think back to your childhood. Remember how much you cared about your friend's opinion of you? No child wants to be made fun of or ridiculed by their peers. It takes strength to risk disapproval.

Parents can offer their children a protective shield against the ridicule of their peers. The first step is to teach kids to believe in the value of their ideas and to ignore what other kids think of them. Children who develop a healthy attitude about the opinions of their peers are learning to believe in themselves. For example: the child who can say, "So what if they don't like the game I invented," will not be swayed by the negative opinions of other children.

Techniques that Teach Original Thinking

What if your child doesn't seem to have original ideas? Or can't ignore the opinions of other kids? Or can't believe in the value of her ideas? Several simple techniques can help.

Attribute Listing

Attribute listing is a method that can be used to increase children's original thinking and to practice searching for original ideas. An advantage of attribute listing is that ideas can be stated, and children can practice original thinking without worrying about evaluation. Furthermore, parents can share in the development of their child's original ideas.

Attribute listing changes the appearance or meaning of an object or thought, and it is a practical activity that focuses on questions. Michael Leboef, author of *Imagineering*, describes how attribute listing develops new ideas for the use of household tools like the screwdriver.[8]

For example, if your child has an interest in hand tools, start by asking several questions.

Ask: "What makes this screwdriver different from other tools?"

Look for answers like: its handle is made of wood, it has a steel shaft, and it is hand operated.

Next ask: "Can you think of ways to improve a screwdriver?"

The purpose is to focus on the attributes your child gives and to improve them. Look at each attribute. If your child mentions the screwdriver's wooden handle, that trait might be made stronger if it is changed to plastic. Or instead of a hand-operated screwdriver it could be changed to battery power.

The idea is to stimulate the thinking of your child. Don't be disappointed if his answers will not turn you into a wealthy entrepreneur. The changes and improvements children make only need to be new and original to them. Children can be encouraged to look at each part of an object, think about why it has to be this way, and how it can be changed.

Forced Relationships

A second technique for developing fresh and original ideas is called *forced relationships*. Using forced relationships requires children to think of a relationship between two unrelated objects or ideas. It also helps them think imaginatively and develops new thinking patterns.

Forced relationships also teaches children to expand their thinking about a familiar object and apply their new ideas to a problem. For example, if children think about tree leaves and a table it might lead to ideas for a table decoration.[9]

If children have a difficult time using their imagination, emphasize building on the ideas of others and withholding evaluation until the flow of ideas is completed. It is OK to encourage outlandish thinking, but hold off on judging the ideas until the evaluation period. This is where the Discovery Checklist (ch. 3) can help. When children bog down, the discovery questions give them a jump start. Useful questions are: Can you take part of it away? Can you multiply or divide it? Can you make it smaller or larger?

The following exercises help you practice attribute listing and forced relationships with your kids. First choose the object for attribute listing, then answer the questions. The object for this exercise is a bicycle.

Attribute Listing

Object: *Bicycle*

Questions:	Answers:
1. How many different ways are there to use a bicycle?	1. _____ _____ _____
2. How is a bicycle different from other things you ride?	2. _____ _____ _____ _____
3. Can you think of ways to improve a bicycle?	3. _____ _____ _____ _____

Now let's try a problem using forced relationships.

Forced Relationships

Objects: *Bicycle and Motorcycle*

Questions	Answers
1. How are a bicycle and a motorcycle alike?	1. _____ _____ _____ _____
2. How can a bicycle be improved by making it more like a motorcycle?	2. _____ _____ _____

To finish the exercise we will use a few of the Discovery Checklist questions to illustrate how they stretch children's thinking. Use the following questions from the Discovery Checklist to solve the problem "How many ways can you think of to improve a bicycle?"

Questions	Answers
1. Can you add something?	1. _____ _____
2. Can you take part of it away?	2. _____ _____
3. Can you make it from different material?	3. _____ _____
4. Can you make it smaller or larger?	4. _____ _____

Summary

Children have unique creative abilities that can be encouraged or squelched. Putting aside the myths about creativity isn't easy, however. If parents put their faith in the myths, they may shortchange their child's natural gifts and abilities. By modeling creative behavior and instructing children in the creative process, parents can give their kids a boost toward reaching their creative potential.

Points to Remember

1. By dispelling the myths about creativity, parents can begin to build a home atmosphere that ignites creative thinking.

2. Creativity is contagious, and many creative adults grew up in creative homes.

3. Watch for your child's flashes of creative talent.

4. Children learn to be persistent by following their parents' example.

5. Ways to help your child develop persistence are:
   - Teach her to finish a task.
   - Leave free time in her schedule.
   - Teach your child to believe in himself.

6. Attribute listing and forced relationships are methods that stimulate creative thinking.

Family Activities

1. Use the following list to practice attribute listing and forced relationships. Three to five minutes should be enough time for each object. Follow the examples given earlier in this chapter.

   computer
   television
   wheel
   shoe
   flashlight
   battery
   hair dryer

2. Ask your child to show how he or she would design and equip a space station. Use the Discovery Checklist to help solve the problem.

Twelve Ways to Help Children Develop Concentration and Persistence

Preschool

1. Know the limits of your child's attention span. Young children can stay with a task for only a few minutes before their attention wanders off.
2. Your child's behavior will tell you when she is ready to go on to something else.
3. If your son asks to help you, give him a task and make sure he completes it.
4. If your daughter hasn't finished a job, call her back and talk about it. If it is important, insist that she finish.

Early Elementary

1. Limit your child's work periods so he can achieve success before he tires.
2. Reduce distractions when your child is reading, solving puzzles, or writing a story. Set a special time each day for your child's creative projects.
3. Provide time for creative thinking activities like music appreciation, drawing, and dramatic play.

4. Reward your child for her accomplishments. Use a magnet to place her poem on the refrigerator door. Read her story to the family.

Late Elementary
1. Let him work on his own. Don't help him unless he asks for it.
2. Be certain your child has a library card and transportation to the library.
3. Be a good model. Explain how long it takes you to accomplish a task and show the completed product.
4. Don't preach a sermon about persistence. Teach by your example.

Notes

1. Michael LeBoeuf, *Imagineering* (New York: McGraw-Hill, 1980).
2. Leslie Dormen and Peter Edidin, "Original Spin," *Psychology Today,* July/August 1989.
3. Andrea Atkins, "The Case for Creativity: Encouraging Our Kids to Think," *Better Homes and Gardens,* April 1989.
4. Lester David, "Strokes of Genius," *Reader's Digest,* June 1990.
5. Julius and Zelda Segal, "Kindle the Creative Spark," *Parents,* February 1990, 80.
6. Ibid.
7. Ibid., 79.
8. LeBoeuf, *Imagineering.*
9. Sidney J. Parnes, "Idea-Stimulation Techniques," *The Journal of Creative Behavior,* 10 (1976).

5

Values:
The Fuel of Creativity

Not long ago my five-year-old granddaughter was showing off what she had learned in kindergarten. She was busy with crayons and paper, writing her name and furiously drawing strange-looking people with stick arms and legs. After working diligently for a few minutes, she skipped over to where I sat and poked the paper in my face.

"Look what I did, Grandpa," she beamed, tripping over my feet in her excitement.

The look on her face was priceless. Her face glowed with the love of learning, with pride in what she had accomplished, and with a desire to excel that I hope will always be there. It wouldn't have taken much to squelch her enthusiasm. If I had told her that human arms don't look like sticks, or that the head of the person she had drawn was nearly as large as its body, she might not have been as eager to show her creative work to me the next time.

What Values Do for Creativity

What happens at home either stimulates creativity or kills it. Teresa Amabile in her book *Growing Up Creative* quotes a study that compares the home of creative and less-creative adolescents.

An important finding of this study is that in creative homes parents have fewer rules, but "present a clear set of values about right and wrong, display those values by their own example, and encourage their children to decide which behavior exemplifies those values."[1]

The research, however, suggests that parents can easily confuse values and rules and place too great an emphasis on rules. In the long run it's the values that your children learn, not the number of rules you enforce, that will help your kids develop creative solutions to tough problems.

The gist of this research should warm the hearts of parents who want their children to reflect God's nature. The moral principles found in the Old and New Testaments are at your fingertips, and children who follow these values will have the background and backbone to refuse to conform to society's mold, because by the "virtue of their creativity they will be a breed apart, and distinctly different."[2]

A New Testament Example

We don't know much about Jesus' family life, but it seems fairly certain that Mary and Joseph gave Him room to be creative and to make His own decisions. We get a glimpse of Jesus as a preadolescent when His family traveled to Jerusalem to celebrate the Feast of the Passover and visit the temple. Apparently, they didn't keep a tight rein on Him because on the way home Jesus' parents didn't miss Him for a day, and it took two more days to find Him.

While He was missing from His family Jesus seemed to demonstrate His ability for creative thinking as He exchanged ideas with the Jewish teachers. Luke 2:41-45 describes how He astonished the temple elders with His understanding of Scripture and the depth of His answers to their questions.

Like many parents, Mary and Joseph didn't understand their child's behavior, but there is no record that they disciplined Him for breaking rules. Scripture tells us that they simply asked, "Son why have you treated us like this?" (v. 48, NIV).

One of the lessons taught by this story may be hard for parents to accept, for it teaches us that sometimes parents must let their children act independently. Jesus' parents didn't try to smother Him with restrictions.

Emphasize Values, Not Rules

Parents can easily get bogged down in rules at the expense of ideals that assist creative development. Rules are a must for a smooth-running family, but parents need to avoid rules that restrict children's thinking and keep them from making decisions on their own. Sometimes values and rules are jumbled and difficult to separate. The following exercise will give you a chance to compare your use of values with the number and kind of rules used in your family. Remember, the final goal is to reduce rules and emphasize moral principles.

Choosing from the sample values below, make a list representing those important to your family. Your list should represent the standards you want for your children, and you are free to pick from the list, add to it, or ignore it:

- Love God
- Tell the truth
- Be considerate of others
- Respect parents
- Respect teachers
- Appreciate money
- Accumulate material goods
- Value hard work
- Value education
- Know how to use power
- Develop self-control
- Value winning

After listing your choice of values, list your family's rules. Here are some suggested rules you might want your children to follow:

- Go to bed on time
- Eat without throwing food
- Watch TV only on the weekends
- Finish homework
- Bathe regularly and wear clean clothes
- Do chores on time without complaining

The third step is to add missing values that you think are important but are not a part of your family's value system. Next, look at your list of rules to see if any can be eliminated. Finally, ask yourself the question, "Do I live up to the standards that I teach my children?"

Values or Rules?

Our family values are:

1. _____
2. _____
3. _____
4. _____
5. _____

Our family rules are:

1. _____
2. _____
3. _____
4. _____
5. _____

Values we want to develop:

1. _____
2. _____
3. _____
4. _____
5. _____

Rules we can eliminate:

1. _____
2. _____
3. _____
4. _____
5. _____

Do I model the values I want my child to learn? How can I improve?

1. _____
2. _____
3. _____
4. _____
5. _____

Keeping a Creative Journal

Lucia Capacchione suggests a method parents can use to help their children develop creative thinking and mature in their understanding of right and wrong. Journal keeping develops children's sense of confidence and security, intensifying their creative thinking. Among other things, a creative journal "provides children with excellent tools for exploring their own personal values, preferences, desires and talents."[3]

Cappacchione has trained many California teachers to use a creative journal in their classes. She says this kind of journaling is suitable for children from kindergarten to sixth grade, but it also has been used with younger and older children. While it has been used extensively in schools, parents also have been trained to use this technique with their children.

> The journal page is like a blank television screen, with the child creating the picture or words on the screen out of his or her own experience and imagination. Journal-keeping encourages thinking and communicating, stimulates creativity, and fosters emotional awareness and expression. It can also be the vehicle for . . . drawing, poetry and autobiographical writing about personal or family values and culture.[4]

Several elements of journal keeping influence and aid the development of creative thinking:

1. It takes the pressure to perform off the child. A basic rule of creative journaling is that no one looks at the journal unless the child gives permission. The child develops his own thinking and states his opinions honestly. Creative journal keeping allows the child to experiment with his own writing and art work. The blank page promotes the child's own thinking.

2. The journal helps the child gather and sort out ideas, and cultivate creative thinking in writing and art. Because the creative journal uses writing and art, the child's verbal and nonverbal imagination, originality, and creativity are stimulated. Before a child tackles a class assignment, writes a letter, or makes a decision, she can write her thoughts in the journal.

3. Keeping a creative journal influences right-brain and left-brain development and helps establish balanced thinking. The combination of art and writing stimulates the child's visual thinking (right brain) and logical thinking (left brain). The daily routine of writing enhances the child's logical left-brain thinking, while the drawing and

art work stimulate right-brain nonverbal thinking and imagination.

Journaling Activities

Capacchione details a variety of uses for the creative journal, but expressing feelings and values is probably one of the most constructive uses of journaling. Here are several instances where writing in a journal helps children:

A family crisis.—It is difficult for children to understand the divorce or separation of their parents or the death of someone they love.

Emotional upheaval.—Often children find changes in classes, grades, schools, or a move to a new neighborhood extremely stressful. Sometimes a move to a new school or neighborhood provokes conflict with new acquaintances.

A new addition to the family.—Children may be upset by a newborn brother or sister. But a grandparent or family friend who moves in for an extended period also can disrupt a child's sense of security.

Capacchione also suggests several writing and art activities for children. Each exercise helps establish a family bond and gives kids opportunities to think and talk about birth, death, changes in the family, and important values. The following statements briefly summarize a few of these creative activities:

1. *The family that plays together.*—First, the child is asked to draw a picture of his family having fun together. Next, he lists the things he likes to do with his family, and finally, he writes about what is happening in the picture.

2. *Family tree.*—The activity begins by asking the child to make a diagram of her family tree and write a short statement about each family member. Parents will need to help younger children or children with poor language skills with the writing. When writing is difficult, the child can draw the tree, and the parent record the necessary information.

3. *A family portrait.*—The child is instructed to draw or paint a portrait including himself, his parents, pets, plants and other individuals he loves. Then he is asked to write about each individual, pet, or plant. In addition to these activities, parents can develop simple writing and drawing exercises that will help their children think about values, and right and wrong behavior.[5]

To launch creative journaling in your family begin with the following steps:

- Supply each participating child with an 8½ by 11-inch notebook filled with unlined white paper. Colored drawing pens, crayons, pencils, or pens are also needed for each child.
- Explain that from time to time you will ask them to write or draw on special topics, but they are free to choose themes, too.
- For the first few times you can assign the topics. Afterwards, as the process catches on, let the children choose what they will write or draw in their journals.

Possible topics include:
- Draw a picture of your family having fun together.
- Write about and illustrate a scene from your favorite book.
- Imagine you're a character in a Bible story. Tell what you like and don't like about where you live.
- Write about "My favorite holiday."
- Write about "What makes me happy."
- Draw a picture of how you feel when you are angry.
- Interview one of your grandparents, and find out about your family's history.
- Imagine you were at your favorite spot. Draw a picture, or write about it.

Respect Creative Thinking

A creative journal is a valuable asset for developing creative thinking skills and family values. But the way you feel about your child's accomplishments also affects his ability to be creative.

Unknowingly, you may signal whether you are for or against your child's ideas and accomplishments. Kids are alert to what you say, to your facial expressions, to your body language, and any of these can signal the way you feel about their ideas and accomplishments.

Parents who are sensitive to the intellectual and emotional needs of their children and reward them for their creativity are promoting creative behavior. Dr. E. Paul Torrance suggests several principles required for rewarding the creative behavior of children.[6]

1. *Respect questions.*—Children have inquiring minds. They love to show off what they know, sometimes with surprising results. An acquaintance of mine likes to tell the story about his three-year-old daughter, who pestered him to test her knowledge. "Ask me a hard question," she nagged.

"OK," her dad said. "What's the capital of Ohio?"

"O," she shot back.

Think of the times your child has worn you out with questions. It's tempting to brush off questions, but if you take the questions seriously, you will give a boost to your son or daughter's self-image.

Be ready, because children ask questions that will set you on your heels. "The trouble is that often the questions come when you're least prepared to answer—or they are so unusual, so unthinkable, that you slam the door on them without thinking."[7]

2. *Value imaginative, unusual ideas.*—Learn to respect not only the questions kids ask, but to appreciate their ideas, too. Children's ideas aren't always brilliant or inventive, and sometimes they are ridiculous. Nevertheless, parents who want their children to think creatively must reward their kids' ideas with respect.

Moms and dads who honestly believe their kids' ideas are valuable will listen more intently to what their children say. The next step is to use these new ideas. Look for ways to show how worthwhile your child's views are. You won't help your child's creative thinking if your reactions to her ideas are:

- This is bad.
- This is good.
- I don't like it.

A better way to show how you feel about the worth of your child's thinking is to say:

- I like this because . . . .
- This could be improved by . . . .
- What will happen if you . . . ?

3. *Hold off on evaluation.*—Evaluation that comes too soon subdues children's thinking. Children need periods of unevaluated time because they show the greatest creativity when they are free to follow an interest important to them. The joy of creative thinking comes when children are motivated and challenged to write a poem, collect bugs, or scribble with a crayon.

The Parent's Role

It is overwhelmingly clear that parents play a specific role in developing their children's creative thinking. Parents promote creative thinking by their stance on values, and their respect for their kids' creative ventures. Creative thinking grows when kids are challenged by a new idea and are given a chance to explore it. The parent's job is to provide the space and time, then watch the results.

Points to Remember

1. Too many rules squelch a child's creativity while emphasizing moral ideals increases creativity.

2. Don't overcontrol your child; instead, trust his decisions.

3. A proper attitude toward your child's ideas will promote creativity.

4. Parents who model the standards they teach are promoting creative thinking.

5. You reward creative thinking by respecting your child's ideas, questions, and need for unevaluated time.

Family Activities

The following activity can be used as a creative journaling exercise or as a separate activity. Ask your child to choose a Bible character and arrange an imaginary interview. Encourage your child to ask the Bible character questions and to imagine the answers he or she will give. The interview may be oral or your child may want to write a script for a newspaper or television interview.

Child's question: ——————————————————————
Character's reply: ——————————————————————
Child's question: ——————————————————————
Character's reply: —————————————————————— [8]

Notes

1. Teresa Amabile, *Growing Up Creative* (New York: Crown, 1989), 104.

2. Howard Hendricks, Mount Hermon Christian Writers Conference, 1991.

3. Lucia Capacchione, *The Creative Journal for Children* (1989): 8.

4. Ibid., 9.

5. Ibid., 65-67.

6. E. Paul Torrance, *Rewarding Creative Behavior* (Englewood Cliffs: Prentice-Hall, 1965).

7. Fredelle Maynard, *Guiding Your Child to a More Creative Life* (Garden City: Doubleday, 1973), 32.

8. Capacchione, 95.

6

Finding the Creative Flash

Sometimes creative solutions to our problems come to us at odd moments and as unexpected breakthroughs. That's the way it was with Monte Unger, a free-lance writer and editor for *Decision* magazine.

Unger's creative light flashed on one day when he was confronted with a problem he couldn't solve. It was his wife's birthday, and he wanted to make her "big-four-O" a happy one. His wife had planned to be away, and he decided to line the sidewalk to their front porch with daisies and put up an enormous, "Happy Birthday," sign.

Anxiety wouldn't let him do it. He worried about what the neighbors would think about the sign and the flowers. Besides, the flowers would cost too much, and he didn't have enough vases to hold them.

Unger's anxiety was blocking a creative solution until he realized that his creative nature came from God. This time he didn't let the problem squash his creativity, and he took an innovative course of action. Here's how he tells it.

> Our sons and I went out into the fields near where we lived and collected dozens of long-stemmed black-eyed Susans. . . . In the basement of our house we found several boxes of old jars that Linda had been collecting—again free!
>
> We filled the jars with water and turned the walkway into a path of flowers. We found a huge sheet of paper, painted our message of love, and taped the sign to the front porch. . . . All of the work was worth it. . . . We had successfully softened her entrance into her forties."[1]

Unger confesses that the truth of his creative breakthrough changed his approach to problems. When he paid attention to his creative light, he found fresh new ways of thinking about raising his kids, planning a birthday party, and having fun.

A Five-Step Creative Process

If you look carefully at Unger's story, you find the recipe for creative thinking. The creative route to a new idea or product operates in the same way for children and adults. For Unger, the creative process followed these steps:

He had a problem.—It was his wife's birthday. He wanted to plan a surprise celebration for her, but his plan was expensive and his neighbors might think he was acting foolishly.

A new idea began to form.—He decided on an innovative action. He finally understood he was God's creation, and he could be creative, too.

He thought of a way to solve his problem.—He substituted black-eyed Susans for nursery flowers and old jars for vases. He decided to paint a "Happy Birthday" sign rather than buy an expensive one.

A time for action.—His sons helped him pick the flowers, fill the jars, and paint the sign.

It was a success.—The idea worked and it was low cost. Unger stopped worrying about the neighbors and enjoyed the birthday celebration.

The creative process that Unger used is the same one parents can use to handle everyday hassles and problems that threaten to disrupt their family. The following is a more detailed version of what takes place when we think creatively.

1. *Finding background information.*—Before your child can think creatively about a task there needs to be preparation time. This is the step in the creative process

where your child is absorbed by his research. You'll recognize this step when he brings home an armload of books on subjects ranging from aliens to zoology. Research is mainly a left-brain task, and it's hard work.

You can help with practical kinds of encouragement. It may be that your kid needs transportation to the library or to an exhibit that interests him. Psychologist Julius Segal puts it squarely on the parents. He says, "To ignite a child's creative zeal, it is essential to find time to go to museums and galleries as well as to shopping malls, to attend craft fairs as well as movies."[2]

2. *Letting ideas form and develop.*—Now the child broods over the information she has gathered. In fact, she may appear to have dropped the project and start another one. But the idea is hatching, her brain is working, and she's getting ready for what comes next.

> The mind is taking those ideas and moving them around, perhaps changing bits and pieces, perhaps adding something you hadn't consciously thought of. When it's time to come back for final planning, the results will be better, more creative than they would have been had you worked through your planning all at one time.[3]

3. *The solution is clear.*—The fun begins and your son or daughter dives in with a frenzy of activity. There is a flash of insight. Don't be surprised when he yells, "Mom, I've got it," because that's what has happened. The problem is solved, it makes sense, and he knows what he wants to do.

4. *Now it's back to work.*—The project or idea must be completed. It is an exciting time for children, and they are caught up in a flurry of activity. If your child is writing a story, he may change the characters or the plot. It all seems to come together and make sense.

5. *Validation is the final step in the creative process.*—It gives the child a chance to look at the completed project

and to evaluate it. This is the time when children ask questions like: Is it a good idea? What should I change? Should I toss it out and try again?

Make the Process Work

What can parents do to help their child's creative thinking flourish? First, don't downplay your influence as a parent because it's in your power to either kill your child's creativity or cause it to flower. Instill in your child the confidence to pursue different paths because "God created me to be creative." By valuing creative thinking, you encourage the creative process and your child's ability to think creatively.

Second, make creativity a top priority in your family. Howard Hendricks, Dallas Theological Seminary professor, believes that thinking creatively is an everyday experience—a life-style. It is a part of the family's daily life and includes everything the family does. If parents are sincere about helping their children become creative thinkers, they will be enthusiastic role models, communicating their joy of creativity while helping their children explore, investigate, and discuss creative ideas.[4]

The steps to a creative solution sometimes blur, but if you think about it, the creative stages are there. Here's an exercise that will help you clarify the steps in your family's creative problem solving.

Follow the outline below to summarize your family's solution to a problem. Fill in the blanks telling how you completed each step in the process. Did you handle the problem creatively or did the creative process break down?

As children grow, they learn to identify and use the steps in the creative process. With the help of their parents, school problems, family rules, getting along with a brother or sister, and any number of other problems can be solved.

Problem:

Step 1. Gathering information about the problem:

Step 2. Thinking about the problem:

Step 3. Clarifying the solution:

Step 4. Working out the solution:

Step 5. Evaluating the solution:

However, a word of caution is necessary. Don't expect your four-year-old to fit into the creative process in the same way that your ten-year-old will. A child's age makes a difference in how he approaches problems and solves them.

A four-year-old can't be expected to have the baseball skills of a fifth-grader. And the same is true of children's creative development. But the ideas still churn in a child's mind, and you can steer his creative thinking if you know the behavior to expect for your child's age and development.

Age Differences

Teresa Amabile's guide to children's creativity gives parents an idea of what to expect at different age levels. If your child doesn't fit precisely into one of these age levels, remember that these are general classifications and depend upon physical, social, and intellectual development. Use the levels to plan and evaluate your child's creative behavior and to plan creative activities.

Check Your Progress

Let's stop and review some facts about creativity and creative thinking, since you still may have misconceptions or questions that bother you. Here are six questions and answers that review information about creativity. Hopefully, they will clear up any questions you have about your child's creative development:

Q. If I smother my child with affection, will his creativity thrive?

A. Experts believe that the opposite happens. An overly affectionate bond between a parent and child will force the child to become dependent and retard a child's creative development.

Q. My child has a mind of her own and doesn't like to be told what to do. Is this a sign of creativity or is she headed for delinquency?

A. An independent child is not the same as an out-of-control, delinquent child. Children should be allowed a reasonable amount of freedom to choose

Age*	Area	Examples of Creative Behavior
2-3	Singing	Inventing melodies or putting their own nonsense words to songs rather than simply repeating songs they have heard.
	Drawing	Playing around with different lines, shapes, and colors.
	Building	Experimenting with various types of structures.
	Playing Instruments	Trying out combinations of sounds on toy instruments or household objects.
4-5	Painting	Combining colors in new ways, using both brushes and fingers.
	Word Play	Playing with the sounds and meanings of words, often while talking to themselves.
	Dancing	Using dance as a way of expressing feeling or experimenting with physical motion.
	Fantasy	Inventing imaginary playmates or assuming the role of pretend characters playing out pretend events.
6-7	Cooking	Experimenting, under adult supervision, with food combinations; using food as an art form.
	Sculpture	Using clay, sand, and other materials to make various shapes.

*Age ranges are approximate averages. Children at each age also show more advanced versions of the creative behaviors typical of the younger ages, and less-developed versions of the creative behaviors typical of older ages.[5]

Age*	Area	Examples of Creative Behavior
	Drama	Making up and acting out plays, including costumes, songs, and dialogue.
6-7	Social Relations	Adopting new and useful solutions to interpersonal conflicts.
8-9	Storytelling	Sustaining a coherent storyline with invented characters and situations.
	Games	Inventing elaborate games with rules and goals.
	Dressing	Deliberately putting together outfits that combine clothing styles in unusual ways.
10-11	Numbers	Playing with ways of using numbers to describe things.
	Language	Creating secret words or languages with siblings or small groups of friends. (This can occur earlier in twins.)
	Visual world	Decorating living environments, often in idiosyncratic ways around themes that hold personal meaning.
12-13	Machines	Studying mechanical and electronic devices, often rebuilding them or using them in new ways.
	Information	Gathering information in logical ways, experimenting, and using inductive and deductive reasoning.
	Writing	Expressing ideas using metaphor and simile, in prose and in poetry.

their activities. For children to become independent, responsible adults, they must be given as
much independence as their age and maturity will
allow.

Q. How can I teach my child to think creatively when
I'm not creative?

A. Repeat over and over, "I am capable of creative
thinking." Creative thinking is not a mystical talent
that blesses a few people; it is a skill that is learned.
Children learn to think creatively when their parents
encourage them to think creatively. You'll probably
discover your own creativity in the process.

Q. My son doesn't seem to know the difference between
work and play. Will he ever be creative?

A. A child who is absorbed in the creative process may
not be aware there is a difference between work and
play. Your child may think his project is so much
fun, it can't be work. Don't forget that playfulness is
a characteristic of creativity.

Q. Isn't rewarding my daughter for her creative ideas a
form of bribery?

A. To reward a child is not bribery. Rewards are earned,
and if used sparingly, they are a useful way to encourage creative behavior. You are the best judge
of your child's behavior. Decide on the type of motivation she responds to and decide on the rewards
you will give. Avoid payment for creative activity,
but bonuses for performance may heighten creativity.[6]

Q. Can my preschool child think creatively?

A. Young children express their creativity differently
than older ones, but the creative flashes are there if
you look for them. Because many parents think of
creativity as a special talent, they may find it hard to
believe that all children, including their own, are creative.

Q. When my son asks dumb questions, should I tell him how stupid they sound?

A. Telling children their ideas are dumb or ridiculous kills creativity. Creative thinking skills are not developed overnight, and it takes hard work and commitment on the part of parents to help each child identify his creative abilities. Children who do not know how to attack a problem may have trouble reaching a creative solution. Parents can help children evaluate their ideas by pointing out the weaknesses in their thinking and encouraging them to move ahead.

Points to Remember

1. The five steps in the creative process are: finding background information, taking time for ideas to form and develop, waiting for a flash of insight, working out a clear solution, and validating the idea.

2. Creative thinking requires a solid background of information.

3. The creative route follows the same steps for children and adults, but don't expect your four-year-old to perform like a ten-year-old child.

4. If parents are enthusiastic role models of creative thinking, creativity will be an everyday family experience.

Family Activities

1. Start a family invention convention. Get the children's ideas. Help them find materials and background information. Guide them through the creative process.

2. Decide how you will model creativity for your children. Make attendance at a children's symphony or other cultural event a regularly scheduled family attraction.

3. Write your own imagineering game around the rules given below. It can be any game you and your children make up. These are the rules for imagineering games:

     a. It is a game where players can pretend. During the game the players sit quietly, in a comfortable position, with their eyes closed.

     b. The leader gives the directions and tells the players what to imagine. Just pretend, don't really do it.

     c. Don't answer questions or speak out when the leader asks you to do something. It's OK to nod your head "yes" or "no."

     d. Don't make the game too long, but adjust the game to the age of the players. The limit for many children is about ten minutes.

Checklist to Improve Imagination

Preschool

1. Make games out of everyday events. If your tot makes noises like a cat or dog, invent a game about animals.
2. Help your child enjoy imaginative play. Plan a mini-drama with your child playing one character and you another. Use hand puppets and other toys that encourage creative thinking.
3. Keep on hand watercolor paints, colored marking pens, plain and colored paper, and other art materials. Allow time to experiment with design and colors. Don't insist that your child draw a house, animal, et cetera.
4. Play music while your child is at play and sing with him. Help him think up a new melody or new words to the song you are singing.

Early Elementary

1. Invent stories built around your child's imaginary playmates. Use cars, trucks, dolls, and other play things to stimulate the stories. Let your child dictate the story and make a book of his stories.
2. Read imagination stretching stories to your child. Make up plays and act them out with other family members.

3. Together dream up an invention. Name the invention and draw a picture of it.
4. Children enjoy playing with codes. Help your child invent a secret code. Check with your librarian for a book of codes.

Late Elementary

1. Begin more detailed story writing. Avoid simply relating events by developing a story plot and characters.
2. Ask your child to invent a video or computer game. Study other computer and video games to determine the necessary components of a game.
3. Ask your child to design "a fun machine." What makes it fun?
4. Design a code using pictures and letters.

Notes

1. Monte Unger, "God is Creator," *Decision*, April 1991, 35.

2. Julius Segal and Zelda Segal, "Kindle the Creative Spark," *Parents*, February 1990, 80.

3. Marlene LeFever, *Creative Teaching Methods* (Elgin: David C. Cook 1986), 28.

4. Howard Hendricks, Mount Hermon Christian Writers Conference, 1991.

5. Teresa Amabile, *Growing Up Creative* (New York: Crown, 1989), 30-32. Used by permission of the author.

6. Jerome Sattler, *Assessment of Children* (San Diego: Jerome M. Sattler, 1988).

7

Motivating
Creative Thinking

When my children were young, on Saturday we all pitched in and cleaned rooms, mowed the lawn, pulled weeds, and finished odd jobs. It irritated me when one of my sons or my daughter found a way to sneak out to a friend's house before all the jobs were finished. I was genuinely upset when I learned that they helped their friends with chores while their jobs were waiting to be completed.

I couldn't figure out, for example, why my children would work willingly at a friend's house pulling weeds and leave our thriving ones begging to be pulled. Too late I learned that I was using the wrong motivators and the other kid's parents knew something that I didn't know. They knew what kind of a payoff it took to get my children to pull weeds.

In case you are wondering, there is a parallel to creative thinking. Unless you find a way to motivate your child's creative thinking, there's a good chance it will not develop. The fact is, some kids are not motivated by long-range rewards, but by immediate, concrete ones.

A Biblical Example

I think the Bible stories of the twins, Jacob and Esau, illustrate the two kinds of motivation. Jacob was a long-range planner who was willing to wait for the reward he knew was coming. Esau wanted instant gratification and didn't worry about the future. Scripture says that Esau, the outdoorsman, came home starved from a hunting trip. He couldn't wait to eat and bargained away his birthright to Jacob for a dinner of bread and lentils (Gen. 25:27-34).

Years later, Jacob met beautiful Rachel and fell in love with her. But Rachel's deceitful father tricked him into marrying an older sister that Jacob didn't love. As a result, Jacob worked fourteen years for his father-in-law before he was allowed to marry Rachel (Gen. 29:15-30).

Two Kinds of Rewards

In many ways children are like these two Bible characters. Some children can look ahead and are motivated by the end results of their creativity. Others can't see beyond the next fifteen minutes and require concrete or extrinsic rewards to get their creative thinking going. To help children blossom we need to know more about what motivates their creativity.

If your child works best for intrinsic rewards, he does something because he genuinely wants to. In this case his reward is his pride in the finished project. And the only reward he needs from you is a hug and an encouraging word. Intrinsic rewards are the goal you, as a parent, are shooting for, but not all children have developed to the stage where they value them.

How can you know if your child is motivated by intrinsic or extrinsic rewards? Here are some examples that will help you understand the difference between these two kinds of motivation. Each example describes a child's behavior, the type of reward that motivates the behavior, and an appropriate parent's response to the behavior.

Child's Behavior	Type of Reward	Parent's Response
1. Works and learns without being pushed.	Intrinsic	Help your child if she asks for it.
2. Works only if rewarded.	Extrinsic	Don't offer rewards. Support your child's ideas. Encourage new interests.

Child's Behavior	Type of Reward	Parent's Response
3. Refuses to go to sleep. Draws, reads, writes by flashlight.	Intrinsic	Give your child more time for special interests.
4. Your child's goal is to make money.	Extrinsic	Emphasize the joy of accomplishment. Check your values.
5. Does the activity if told he must do it. Wants to please you.	Extrinsic	Is the activity hard or boring? Try to build self-confidence.
6. Enjoys a challenge	Intrinsic	Respect your child's ideas. Give her room to fly.
7. Afraid to start something new. Wants you to tell him how to do it. Worries it's not good enough.	Extrinsic	Your child may be unsure of his abilities. Don't criticize, but praise.

Decide on the Best Rewards

It isn't enough to recognize the different effects of intrinsic and extrinsic motivation. The next step is to decide on the kind of motivation that suits your child best and go on from there.

When I was working as a public school psychologist, we held weekly meetings to discuss the children who weren't successful in school. In a nutshell, many of these children weren't interested in anything their parents or teachers suggested, resulting in a decrease in their creativity. Often their parents said something like, "He (she) is driving me crazy. I've tried everything and nothing works."

I think the answer for these children's poor motivation is that they do not care for intrinsic rewards. Rather, they want something they can touch, feel, and spend. For most of these children intrinsic rewards are meaningless, their inner motivation is weak, and other kinds of rewards are needed to heighten their creative interests.

Psychologist Jerome Sattler, writing about the enhancement of children's creativity, says,

> When a high initial level of intrinsic interest is not present, efforts should be made to enhance the child's interest. In such cases, it may be necessary to offer a reward to encourage the child to engage in the activity. As interest develops, rewards can be withdrawn or be made less salient. At both home and school, reinforcements should be tailored to the individual child's level of interest and ability.[1]

Rules for Rewarding Children

Let's assume that your child is one who doesn't seem to care about rewards for good thinking. If this is the case, there are some basic facts and rules about rewards that you need to know.[2]

Rule 1: Give positive recognition immediately. Pay attention to your child's accomplishments and show your approval. Be alert to your child's successes, and have something good to say about what she has achieved. For example:

A child made her lunch without being asked and included a piece of fruit instead of a candy bar.

Mom: "Good job, Judy. You made a healthy lunch today."

Child: "Oh, thanks, Mom. I'll make my lunch tomorrow, too."

Rule 2: Don't hold off on giving positive recognition. Saving up on positive responses only causes the child's progress to slow down. A parent-child dialogue without a positive reward might go like this:

Child: "See, Mom, I've finished my drawing."

Mom: "That's nice, I'll look at it later when I'm not busy."

Child: (To herself) "Forget it. It stinks anyway."

Two things happen when parents delay rewards even for a little while. First, the behavior you want to encourage stops happening, and second, the child's progress is slowed.

Rule 3: Aim your child's rewards toward what is important to her. Find out what your child likes, and if you don't know, ask her. Children work energetically to earn something important to them.

Child: "Dad, when I finish my science project can I play my video games?"

Dad: "Video games are a waste of time. Find something better to do."

Child: (Again to herself) "Anything's better than this stupid science."

Rule 4: Don't overlook a good accomplishment and don't reward behavior you don't want. The principle of this rule is consistency. Good things aren't going to happen if you stick to the agreement one day and forget about it for the next two days. Ron Carter says, "Parents must set up predictable reinforcers for kids. If we want consistently good performance from the child, our behavior must also be consistent."[3]

Perhaps this is a typical mother-daughter dialogue:

Child: "Here's a poem I wrote for you, Mom. How does it sound?

Mom: "This is great. I'll put it on the frig door. Why don't you play video games for an extra thirty minutes today?"

Child: (To herself) "I'm going to write more poems."

A Reward for the Wrong Behavior

Any time you recognize creative thinking, be positive, letting your child know that you approve. You can't always be with your child to observe what's happening, but when you see tangible evidence of creative behavior, reward it. Of course, this isn't always easy to do. Parents aren't with their children twenty-four hours a day. And sometimes a creative child twists things around so that you end up rewarding the wrong behavior.

Behavioral psychologists John and Helen Krumboltz gave an example of a mom who unwittingly rewarded her daughter, Jeanine, for using her creativity to get out of cleaning a messy room. This is her mother's side of the story:

> When Jeanine was told to clean her room, she half-heartedly picked up dirty clothes and ran the vacuum until she convinced her mom that she was hard at work cleaning and straightening. It wasn't long, however, before she stopped working and did what she wanted to do.
>
> Later she would come out smiling with some ingeniously constructed junk sculpture, some witty little poem or drawing. I would simply have to admire and exclaim over her creative production.[4]

Jeanine's mother felt trapped. She was impressed by her daughter's creativity, but she also was furious because she ended up cleaning the room. She failed to insist on a neat and clean room, thinking she would squelch her daughter's creativity. Jeanine wouldn't have fooled her mother if her mom had paid more attention to her daughter's behavior. The problem was solved by paying close attention to what Jeanine did and the rewards she received.

There were at least two steps this mom could have taken to stop Jeanine's disobedience and help develop her creativity.

1. She could have insisted on work time and art time.

2. Or she could have reinforced Jeanine's creative efforts to make her room attractive.

What Would You Do?

Now let's try some true-to-life children and test your ability to reward their creative thinking. I will give you examples of several children who are not using their creative abilities. How would you help them?

For each problem try to answer the following questions:

- What is the specific problem?
- What behavior do you want to strengthen or weaken?

- When do you want the behavior to occur?
- What reward will you use?[5]

1. Rhonda is an excellent reader but only reads the comics. How will you help her increase her interest in reading?

2. Joseph's music teacher says he has potential as a trumpet player, but he refuses to practice. How will you help him?

3. Georgia is shy, and she won't speak up in class. You know she has good ideas. How will you get her to say what she thinks?

4. Your three-year-old son scribbles on the wall instead of his coloring book. How will you teach him the difference?

Now, think of a problem that is keeping your child from showing creative potential. Follow these steps and try to determine the best way to reward your child for creative behavior.

What is the problem?_____

What behavior do you want to strengthen or weaken?

When do you want the behavior to occur?_____

What reward will you use?_____

Aim for Intrinsic Motivation

Rewards play an important part in developing creativity and creative thinking. The most creative products have probably come from individuals who have been motivated by intrinsic goals or rewards. Rewards, such as the joy of accomplishment, respect, and fun, are intrinsic motivators.

It would be nice if all children were equally excited by intrinsic motivation. But some aren't, and they need something more tangible to get them started thinking creatively. Extrinsic rewards aren't bribes. They simply give the child the kind of reward he wants for creative thinking. As he becomes more experienced in the creative thinking skills, his rewards will change.

Concrete rewards are "merely a temporary expedient to get the behavior started. . . . A shift from a concrete reward to a less tangible one is a step toward gradually helping the child become independent of external rewards."[6]

Points to Remember

1. Not all children are alike. Some require tangible rewards to motivate creative thinking.

2. Research shows that intrinsic rewards motivate the child to creative thinking.

3. Children who respond to outside pressure are less creative than children whose rewards are interest, enjoyment, and satisfaction.

4. Decide whether your child is motivated by intrinsic or extrinsic rewards and choose the best reward for your child.

5. Tailor children's rewards to their level of interest and ability.

Family Activities

The following activities are designed to encourage children's intrinsic motivation:

1. Sit down with each child in your family and talk about his or her accomplishments. Look at the papers

brought home from school. If Jimmy is excited about astronomy, listen to him and encourage him.

2. Set a regular time for your children to work on fun projects. Don't attach any strings to this time. Let the kids know that the time is set aside for working on their favorite enterprise.

3. Downplay competition. Don't make comparisons between your child's work and other children's accomplishments.

Checklist for Building Enthusiasm

Preschool
1. Talk about interesting subjects. Discuss topics new to your child.
2. Have a good selection of children's books at home. Make regular trips to the public library. Set a time each day for reading to your toddler.
3. Plan daily excursions and talk over your experiences.
4. Use the television as a teaching station. Check the schedule for educational programs. Set a limit on other programs your child watches.

Early Elementary
1. Let your children see your enthusiasm for learning. Talk about new things you have learned. Show your child where you work and explain what you do.
2. Plan a family field trip to explore historic places. Build a file of information about your visits and keep it with other reference material.
3. Introduce your child to a wide variety of cultural activities. Visit museums, musical events, and children's theater.

Late Elementary
1. Continue with activities mentioned previously that are appropriate for your child's age level.
2. This is a critical age for creative development. If you can't answer his questions, help him find where to get the answers.

3. Be certain that your child has the study and research skills necessary to find the information he wants. Does he know how to use the library card catalog system or computer data base?

Notes

1. Jerome Sattler, *Assessment of Children* (San Diego: Jerome M. Sattler, 1988), 683.

2. Ron Carter, *Help! These Kids Are Driving Me Crazy* (Champaign: Research Press, 1972), adapted from pages 26-40.

3. Ibid., 35.

4. John Krumboltz and Helen Krumboltz, *Changing Children's Behavior* (Englewood Cliffs: Prentice-Hall, 1972), 101-2.

5. Carter, 26-40.

6. Krumboltz and Krumboltz, *Changing Children's Behavior*, 111-12.

8

Creative, Gifted, and Talented Kids

Mike and Mary were confident that their first-grade daughter was gifted. Katrina began writing when she was four years old. Her lively stories were filled with humor. When she wasn't writing, she used colored felt-tip pens to illustrate her stories. The characters she painted weren't the usual stick figures drawn by young children. Instead of arms protruding from a too large head and a belly button decorated body, her drawings were two-dimensional and lifelike.

Mary and Mike weren't surprised when they got the letter from Katrina's teacher with the nomination form for the school's gifted program. The letter said that children selected for the program "possess a capacity for excellence far beyond that of other students of the same age." *Wow,* Katrina's parents thought. *What a great opportunity for our daughter!*

But their joy turned sour two or three weeks later when they received another letter from her teacher. This time the letter started by saying, "We regret that Katrina has not qualified for the gifted program."

Mary and Mike couldn't believe it. What about Katrina's stories? The way she made them laugh? Her imagination? Weren't these signs of her giftedness?

Children's Abilities Fool Adults

Parents are often confused by terms like "gifted," "talented," and "creative." There is an overlap in these abilities, and some experts lump gifted, talented, and creative children into one classification.

Katrina's story illustrates the difference between many creative and gifted children. Sometimes a child may be intellectually gifted or talented but not very creative. Other children may be creative but not do well on IQ tests. Katrina was highly creative. But her IQ score wasn't in the top 2 percent of children her age, and she didn't qualify for the class.

Children sometimes fool us. The child we think is creative because of high IQ, high grades, and good behavior may be less creative than the child whose grades are average. Experience has shown that there are differences in behavior, grades, and problem-solving skills between highly intelligent and highly creative children.

Selma Wasserman, a professor of education at Simon Fraser University in British Columbia, wrote about the dead end she ran into trying to get gifted children to think creatively.[1]

She was asked to demonstrate her methods of teaching children to think creatively to a group of California teachers. The lesson went downhill from the start. The gifted and talented pupils were reserved and seemed anxious, perhaps because a large group of teachers was watching. Wasserman skipped to a question she thought would get the demonstration rolling. Here is what happened.

"How do you suppose birds learn to fly?" Wasserman asked.

"What do you mean?" asked a boy.

"I don't understand what we are supposed to do," said a girl, fidgeting uncomfortably in her chair.

"We haven't studied birds yet," responded a studious-looking child near the front of the room.

It seemed to be a stalemate. Wasserman continued to try to tap the creative-thinking abilities of these kids without success. And the kids tried to manipulate her into telling them the right answers to her questions.

That afternoon Wasserman saw a different group of children. They were labeled low achievers, but they jumped at the chance to wrestle with her question, "How could you weigh a giraffe?"

Perhaps the most intriguing answer was "I'd get a big truck and fill it with food that giraffes like to eat. Then I'd weigh the truck. Then I'd hide inside of it and call, 'Here, giraffe. Here, giraffe.' When he got inside, I'd slam the doors and weigh the truck again."[2]

Why were the low achievers able to outthink a group of gifted children? After going back and talking to each group, Wasserman thought she knew the answer. First, the low achievers' out-of-school activities required high-level creative problem solving. They were talented at solving day-to-day problems. Second, the gifted children attended music lessons and French lessons and did enormous amounts of homework. They were experienced at figuring out expectations, performing school-related tasks, and solving single-answer problems, but not problems that demanded creative solutions.[3]

The first group described by Professor Wasserman was a small sample of high-IQ children who seemed to lack matching creative-thinking skills. In fact, creativity runs the whole gamut of intelligence. Experts say that while some children are smart and creative, other children may have IQs far above other kids but lack creativity.

Psychologist Jerome Sattler explains the distinction between gifted, talented, and creative children,

> Giftedness refers to distinctly above-average competence in one or more ability domains, whereas talent refers to distinctly above average competence in one or more fields of human performance. . . . Primary determinants of creativity are abilities (intelligence and originality), motives (need for achievement and striving for novelty), and temperament traits (independence of judgment and tendency to dominate). Some minimum level of intelligence is likely required for creative performance.[4]

Traits that Overlap and Separate

Paul Janos and Nancy Robinson, University of Washington professors, point out that the traits that overlap between gifted and creative children and the traits that separate them. Overlapping characteristics are:

- Intellectual curiosity and a questioning attitude
- Periods of intense concentration
- Broad interests
- Independence of judgment

Traits that separate creative children from gifted ones are:

- Intuition
- Flexibility
- Social poise
- Unconcern for social norms
- A sense of being creative[5]

Another group of researchers found that highly intelligent and highly creative fifth-grade boys and girls also had high levels of self-confidence, interest in schoolwork, and popularity with their peers. Children that were high in intelligence but low in creativity were interested in academic work, but were cool and aloof socially even when other children tried to be friendly. Also, they were intolerant of unusual, unconventional ideas.[6]

Many definitions seem to focus on gifted or creative children, and it is difficult to see where talented children fit into the picture. Talented children have a special gift that may or may not be developed. Parents probably are the first to notice that their child has a special flair for music, dancing, telling stories, or dramatics. These talents spring from the child's interests and are a mixture of giftedness and creativity. Here are some examples of talented children:

- The child who makes up new words for familiar tunes, comes up with original tunes or has an extraordinary sense of pitch is talented musically.

- The boy or girl who enjoys drawing with colored chalks may be expressing a talent for art.
- The child who makes up stories and acts them out is expressing an acting talent.

Unravel the Differences

Here are five scenarios based on actual children that may help to unravel the differences between gifted, creative, and talented children. First read the examples. Next, use what you know about gifted and creative children to answer the quiz at the end of each example. The correct answer and an explanation follow each question.

1. Jill began reading at two or three years of age. Her parents didn't remember encouraging her to read, but they read Bible stories and children's stories each day to her. As a three-year-old she memorized Bible verses and explained their meanings. Before kindergarten, she spent hours thumbing through the volumes of a children's encyclopedia. Her kindergarten teacher was amazed at Jill's emotional, social, and mental maturity.

Jill is: a. gifted, b. talented, c. creative, d. gifted and talented.

Jill is gifted. Her personality traits are similar to many gifted children. Gifted children often learn to read without formal instruction. By the time Jill entered kindergarten, she was reading several grades above that level.

2. Jeff's second-grade teacher sighed with relief when he was safely out of the classroom at the end of the day. He could be counted on to drop papers, trip over a chair, or tip his chair over backward at least once a day. She was surprised at his independence and his curiosity about mechanical things. In spite of his klutzy behavior, his classmates liked him for his zany ideas and off-the-wall questions.

From the information you have about Jeff he is: a. very bright, b. average, c. creative.

It's easy to focus on certain behaviors and ignore others. Jeff's poor large-muscle control is characteristic of his age, and it has nothing to do with the creativity he shows. His zany ideas and questioning nature are signs of creative thinking.

3. Margaret is home teaching her third-grade twins, Theresa and Tiffany. They are identical except for their personalities. While attending public school, the school psychologist gave both girls an individual intelligence test. Their scores were nearly identical and each scored in the very superior classification.

Tiffany's intuition was astonishing, and her understanding of ideas seemed to come out of the blue. But the opposite was true of Theresa. It was easy to see her high ability, but sometimes she seemed one way in her thinking. Kids were always hanging around Tiffany, but Theresa had a "take-it-or-leave-it" attitude about friends.

Theresa and Tiffany are: a. gifted and creative, b. gifted, c. only Tiffany is gifted and creative.

Both girls are gifted. Your answer was correct if you said that Tiffany was gifted and creative. Theresa was as bright as her twin sister, but she didn't have the same creative traits.

4. Jake was a disappointment to his parents. In the primary grades he was a free spirit. He liked new experiences, and on his report cards his teachers underlined and commented on his creativity. This changed about the fourth grade, and by the seventh grade he was a different kid. Jake followed rules without question and worried himself sick if his homework wasn't complete and perfect.

Jake's story shows: a. a drop in his creativity, b. that he was never creative, c. that he is as creative now as he was in the primary grades.

Research shows that as kids grow older they often become less creative. Experts say that creativity flourishes in the primary grades, but many children experience a drop in their creative thinking during the fourth and seventh grades. Jake's primary teachers weren't mistaken.

He was creative. His story illustrates the drop in creative thinking some children experience as they progress through the grades.

5. There isn't a school day that fifth-grader Sheila doesn't enjoy. After school her mom is mobbed by Sheila and her friends. Somehow they get their homework done while talking, watching TV, and snacking on chocolate chip cookies. Sheila's favorite hobby is painting landscapes with her watercolors. Her school grades are average, or a little better, and her achievement tests scores are at grade level.

Sheila is: a. gifted and talented, b. gifted and creative, c. average, d. average and creative.

Sheila is a happy, active child. Her report card may show she is average, but she is creative. Her love for painting is an expression of her creative talent in art, and she should be encouraged to continue.

A Special Challenge

Often a child's natural gifts are clearly recognizable. For example, the average child doesn't learn to read at two or three years of age, even with the help of TV programs like "Sesame Street," and "The Electric Company." To be the parent of a child who is creative, gifted, and talented is a challenge. These kids are fun, but they keep you on your toes with enough surprises to erase boredom and assure a lively household.

Two cautions are necessary. Creative children who are gifted and talented may find activities suited for the average child uninteresting and tedious. Activities should be geared to your child's intelligence and skill. Also, remember not to be misled if your child seems to have a superior grasp of facts. Knowledge by itself doesn't mean a child is gifted or creative. Look for imagination, love of work, eagerness to be involved, and an appetite for training or improving a talent. When you see the glimmerings of creativity, cultivate and nurture it.

Points to Remember

1. Not only high IQ children are creative. Intelligence tests are poor measures of creativity.

2. The relationship between good grades and creativity is low.

3. Gifted and talented children may need training to improve their creative thinking.

4. There is an overlap between the skills and personality traits of gifted and creative children.

5. Distinctive traits of creative children are intuition, flexibility, social poise, and lack of concern for social norms.

6. Talented children have special gifts in fields of human performance that require nurturing and cultivating.

Family Activities

1. Plan family music programs. Music lessons aren't necessary unless your child is willing to practice and is the correct age for beginning an instrument.

2. Look for music events that will develop your child's lifelong enjoyment of music.

3. Tape your child's drawings or sport clippings to the door of the refrigerator.

4. Tell Bible stories and role play favorite passages.

5. Ask your child questions similar to ones asked by Selma Wasserman. For example:
   • How do you suppose . . . ?
   • How could you weigh a . . . ?

Try for a lively discussion, and ask your child to illustrate the answers.

Ways to Develop Independence

Preschool

1. Don't overreact when your toddler says "no." He is trying to be more independent. Be certain discipline is necessary before you administer it.

2. Offer your child choices. For example, ask, "Which cookie do you want?"

3. Don't confine your toddler, but allow him to explore new territory.
4. Remember that striving to be independent is part of your child's normal development.
5. When your child makes a decision, insist that he stick by it.

Early Elementary
1. Let your child express his ideas. Don't belittle them.
2. Let your child plan short family excursions.
3. Encourage him to look for alternate ways of doing things.
4. Encourage your child to think of more than one way to solve a problem. Try out the solutions to see if they work.

Late Elementary
1. Increase the amount of responsibility you give your child.
2. Develop a sense of trust. Don't ask for every detail of his daily schedule.
3. Support your child when he wants to do something out of the ordinary.
4. Talk about Bible stories where the main character refused to conform and follows God's command.

Notes

1. Selma Wasserman, "The Gifted Can't Weigh the Giraffe," *The Phi Delta Kappan*, May 1982, 621.
2. Ibid.
3. Ibid.
4. Jerome Sattler, *Assessment of Children* (San Diego: Jerome M. Sattler, 1988), 684.
5. Paul Janos and Nancy Robinson, "Psychosocial Development in Intellectually Gifted Children," in *The Gifted and Talented Developmental Perspectives* (American Psychological Association: Washington, 1985), 179.
6. Ibid.

9

A Good Laugh Helps

Tom Mullen, author of *Laughing Out Loud*, says,

Parents usually recognize a happy child when they see, hear, and clean up after one. Spilled milk is regarded by few children as a calamity. . . . Children teach us that pleasant things are to be enjoyed and disagreeable things, so long as they don't 'spoil the fun,' acquire a pleasant flavor and provoke a laugh.[1]

Even if some of the humor in your child's jokes escapes you, humor plays a major part in the development of imagination and self-expression. Don't expect, however, to understand or cherish every joke or riddle your child springs on you. Children develop a sense of humor early and sometimes what they think is funny isn't comical, at least from an adult's point of view.

Tiny Tots' Humor

Beginning with infants and toddlers, kids find doing something the wrong way hilarious. For instance there is the game, "Drop It," that tiny kids seem to learn without coaching. I've watched my children and grandchildren play this game, and nearly every parent at some point has been an unwilling partner in the game. "Drop It" starts when your infant grabs a feeding spoon full of strained liver, looks you straight in the eye, and tosses it over the side of the high chair. Amazingly, some parents aren't aware of the game until the spoon hits the floor three or four times.

Older children enjoy jokes, surprises, and humor, too. For example, three-and-four-year-old children enjoy the joke about the mamma hummingbird and the baby hummingbird. It goes like this:

One day the mamma bird decided her baby hummingbird was old enough to fly, and she pushed him out of the nest. Too late the mamma bird watched him flutter down into the grass because he couldn't fly.

"Now do you know how a teeny-tiny hummingbird calls his mom? (Ask this in a whisper). He says (now boom it out), 'Hey, Mom!'"[2]

Humor Saved the Day

Sometimes a joke like the baby hummingbird is funny enough to make your home ring with laughter and cause your spouse and kids to go around the house booming out, "Hey Mom." But jokes aren't the only way humor is expressed. A comical incident can give birth to sidesplitting laughter as the inner kid wins out and mom, dad, and the children collapse laughing.

Occasionally kids' jokes and riddles will rescue a bad situation and turn it into a good one. When our kids were beginning school, we had a favorite book of children's riddles that I was forced to read over and over. The laughter generated by this book was contagious, and the kids' humor usually caused one or the other of our boys to fall over laughing. In fact, one weekend the riddle book saved us from an embarrassing episode.

While attending graduate school, I met an Iranian student and his sister and invited them to our home to meet my family and stay for dinner. It was a great chance to get acquainted, except they arrived on the wrong Saturday afternoon.

While my wife and I huddled in the corner of the kitchen and tried to figure out what to do, the kids corralled our guests and began reading jokes and riddles to them. My sons' laughter was catching, and soon our guests were laughing at the kids' jokes, too. What began as a high-stress situation became a pleasant family memory.

Humor and Creativity

Don and Alleen Nilsen, experts on children's humor and directors of WHIM (World Humor and Irony Membership), believe that humor supports creative development. According to the Nilsens, children's creativity develops as their sense of humor grows. As a child's humor forms a partnership with his creative imagination, the child's ability to express himself improves.

Before parents can use humor to help their child's creativity mature, it is essential to know what makes children laugh. The Nilsens give examples of several kinds of children's humor. See if you recognize some of the jokes and hidden messages in the following illustrations.[3]

1. *Victim jokes and riddles.*—In this type of humor the child's hostility is hidden in a kind of game. The victim is enticed into following a word pattern. The game is to try and get the other child to attack himself. "Children will often get the victim involved in a game that will require the victim to respond without thinking . . . and to make the victim request punishment."[4]

You probably recall some victim jokes or riddles from your childhood. Here's one I used on my brother.

Child: I saw a dead horse on the street. I won it.
Victim: I two it.
Child: I three it.
Victim: I four it.
Child: I five it.
Victim: I six it.
Child: I seven it.
Victim: I ate it.

The instigator's joy is complete if the victim is fooled into saying that he ate the dead horse. But the victim may turn the tables by responding: "I jumped over the dead horse and you ate it."

The following is another example of a hostile riddle. It starts when a child says:

"Adam and Eve and Pinch Me went down to the river to swim. Adam and Eve were drowned. Who was saved?" The victim, trying to show his intelligence, answers, "Pinch Me." The pinching attack follows.

2. *Social Jokes.*—Many of these jokes take the form of insults. It might be a personal slur, attacking another child's appearance, a sexist slur, or an antischool, anti-teacher slur. Even harmless rhymes are potentially hostile or insulting. There are a myriad of endings to the following rhyme, and some are meant to attack or insult. How many other endings do you remember for "Roses Are Red"?

> Roses are red.
> Violets are blue.
> Honey is sweet
> And so are you.

Here are a few traditional rhymes meant to be slurs:

> Cry baby, cry
> Stick your finger in your eye.
> Tell your mother it wasn't I.

> No more teachers.
> No more books.
> No more teachers'
> Dirty looks.

Kids like to build jokes around their teacher's name, but for the unpopular teacher a play on names can be insulting. Most teachers, however, bear up under a friendly name change like the one used by a group of Miss Pastorini's fifth-grade students. Behind her back she was known as "Miss Pass the Donuts."

3. *Humorous folk tales are used by children to establish their equality or superiority.*—According to the Nilsens, children are comforted and reassured when they hear stories about "morons" and the "village idiot."

An example of this kind of story is the one about the silly girl that no one wanted to marry. The only prospect which she had decided not to marry her unless he could find three sillier people.

He started his search, and soon found a man foolish enough to try and load a wagon of walnuts with a fork. Her suitor continued on until he met a farmer who wanted his pig to eat acorns but couldn't figure out why the porker wouldn't climb an oak tree.

Finally, he knew what his decision would be when he found a man with his pants stretched between two trees. This witless fellow climbed one of the trees and tried to put his pants on by jumping from a branch into the legs of his trousers (this required skill and bravery). Of course, the happy man could hardly wait to see his captivating future bride.

Judging from Jennifer Owlsby's essay, "A Handy Guide to Grown-ups," she would catch the humor in the tale of the "Silly Bride." Her creative imagination and sense of humor go hand in glove when she writes:

> Adults are not just big children. They think and act differ-
> ently. . . . For instance, when you were four you probably
> couldn't see over the edge of the kitchen sink. When you
> get bigger you can see right down into it. So you know
> what washing dishes is like. This is fun at first. . . . If you
> were twice as high as you are, elevators would not frighten
> you because you would not have your head pressed be-
> tween people's stomachs.[5]

Recognize Bad Humor

Each day children are bombarded with all kinds of humor. A certain amount of antagonistic joking between siblings or friends is healthy. But hostile, destructive, or dirty jokes shouldn't be tolerated.

There is a yardstick for measuring the quality of your kid's jokes which can be found in Jesus' daily relationships. Jesus wasn't humorless; He used humor every day as He taught the people who came to Him. Instead of hostility, insults, or putting someone down, Jesus used humor to teach and heal.

Elton Trueblood says, "The humor of Christ is employed, it would appear, only because it is a means of calling attention to what would, without it, remain hidden or unappreciated. Truth and truth alone, is the end."[6]

Even young children are adept at seeing the humor in some of Jesus' teaching. Trueblood tells about reading the seventh chapter of Matthew's Gospel to his four-year-old son. As a conscientious parent, he hoped to impress on his son the truth in the parable. The solemn atmosphere was wrecked when the youngster began to laugh.

> He laughed because he saw how preposterous it would be for a man to be so deeply concerned about a speck in another person's eye, that he was unconscious of the fact his own eye had a beam in it. Because the child understood perfectly that the human eye is not large enough to have a beam in it, the very idea struck him as ludicrous.[7]

Fun and Horseplay

A home that honors humor and creativity is a lively place to live. Mullen says, "Parents can positively affect the tone of the family if fun and horseplay are not only allowed but encouraged. Children usually rejoice in healthy teasing and, in fact, may feel excluded if left out."[8]

Parents who share and enjoy humor with their children form a special bond and feel a sense of camaraderie. Being a parent doesn't mean you can't see the funny side of life. Here are some suggestions if you want to increase the use of humor in your home. This isn't an all-inclusive list, and you can probably think of other ways to use humor at home.

• *Have fun together.*—It will make life easier, and your kids won't forget the good times. Start by appointing the family jokester to the role of "Head of Horseplay." It might even be you or your spouse. Your choice may be a kid like Tom Mullen's daughter Martha. He tenderly remembers her as the daughter who put vaseline on her parents' bedroom doorknob and left artificial vomit on the porches of paper route customers.

• *Be a home that honors laughter and refuse to let TV be your guide to family fun.*—A smile, plus a funny comment, often soothes hurt feelings and gets kids back on track. Where threats won't work, humor sometimes will. It is a far more pleasant way to get your child to do distasteful chores.

• *Develop an atmosphere of good humor.*—This doesn't mean let your kids run wild, but even discipline can be handled with good humor. Have an attitude that says, "life is serious but not depressing."[9]

A Way of Life

Why not let humor, off-the-wall ideas, and respect for creative thinking be a way of life for your child? As a parent, you may miss some of the kids' humor that springs up, but your child won't miss a bit of it. Toddlers and up understand and enjoy the humorous and sometimes not so humorous things that happen at home. Parents who watch and listen to their children will find out how entertaining they can be.

Teach your kids to use Christ's example of humor as the yardstick for their jokes. Jesus never used humor to hurt or put down His disciples or His enemies. It's OK if your child loves horseplay and turns a serious discussion into a joke session if it's uplifting comedy, not humor that humiliates someone.

Family comedy is a treasure house of fun and good memories. As your child learns to express herself, good jokes and clean humor go hand in hand with your child's creative imagination. Keep humor free of hostility and free of insults. Keep it healthy and fun.

Points to Remember

1. Even very young children enjoy humor. Tailor the humor you use to your child's age and development.

2. If your child asks, read her favorite joke or riddle book over and over.

3. Be careful that your child isn't using humor at the expense of other children. Don't allow humor that victimizes, insults, or in some way hurts another child's feelings.

4. Humor is a way to make family life more enjoyable. You will hear less about boredom if your kids are having fun at home.

5. Jesus was not humorless. Young children can understand the humor in His parables.

6. Use Christ's humor as an example of good humor.

Family Activities

1. Read nonsense rhymes to your preschool child. When your tot becomes familiar with several rhymes, say the first lines of the rhyme and together make up a new ending.

2. Plan a family comedy night. Let each family member tell a favorite joke or riddle. Don't always start with mom or dad, but share the opening spot.

3. Present the riddle, "Who was the first skin diver?" (answer: the mosquito.) Ask your children to explain why the riddle is funny. Make up other humorous riddles.

4. Protect and encourage humor in your family by:
   - Reading funny stories together.
   - Laughing with your children and letting them play simple jokes on you.
   - Make an April Fools' day painting of something funny or impossible.

5. Play with words until a new vocabulary or humorous language is developed.

6. Susan Amerikaner suggests making up riddles as a method for developing language skills and creative thinking. A riddle can be constructed by using pairs of homonyms, words that sound alike. *Pail* and *Pale* are homonyms. Make a list of homonyms and create some riddles. "Why is a ghost like a small bucket?" (Answer: Because they're both a little pale/pail).[10]

Ways to Increase Humor and Playfulness

Preschool
1. Laugh together when something funny happens. Don't make fun of your child's behavior, but laugh with him about it.
2. Look for humor in everyday situations. Funny things happen that you can share with your preschooler.
   a. Make a joke when your child puts her arm in the wrong sleeve or a shoe on the wrong foot.
   b. Watch for her expressions of humor.
3. Laugh when your tot plays a joke on you.
4. Read children's riddle and joke books with your child. Let her change the endings of jokes and riddles.

Early Elementary
1. Share family jokes.
2. Act out humorous scenes and tape record or video-tape them.
3. Start your home joke library.
4. Don't be too strait-laced; loosen up and have fun with your children's jokes and funny behavior.

Late Elementary
1. Draw a picture of the funniest thing that ever happened.
2. Have a joke-of-the-week bulletin board.
   a. Choose the best jokes.
   b. Let one of the children clip a favorite from the comics.
3. Let the child who writes a funny story or joke read it to the rest of the family.

Notes

1. Tom Mullen, *Laughing Out Loud* (Richmond, Indiana: Friends United Press, 1989), 23.

2. Kent Garland Burtt, *Smart Times* (New York: Harper and Row, 1984), 98.

3. Don and Alleen Pace Nilsen, "Parenting Creative Children: The Role and Evolution of Humor," *The Creative Child and Adult Quarterly* 12 (1987).

4. Ibid., 55.

5. Mullen, 118.

6. Elton Trueblood, *The Humor of Christ* (New York: Harper and Row, 1964), 52.

7. Ibid., 9.

8. Mullen, 17.

9. Ibid., 117-19.

10. Susan Amerikaner, *101 Things to Do to Develop Your Child's Gifts and Talents* (New York: Tom Doherty Associates, Inc., 1989), 69.

10

Where's the Proof?

A few years ago a television commercial swept through America. The commercial featured an eighty-year-old woman, critically eyeing skimpy meat patties on a row of hamburger buns. "Where's the beef?" she demanded.

The lady required proof, and the same type of question is a valid one to ask about creative thinking. For example, where's the proof that creative training makes a difference in a child's life? And will my creative child become a creative adult?

I want to underline the important part parents play in their child's creative development. A child's creativity is more likely to grow if his parents highlight imaginative thinking. Popular creative-thinking programs for adults accentuate many of the same skills that children's programs seek to develop. When children are trained to use their imaginative thinking abilities, they will have the adult skills necessary for creative problem solving.

Becoming Creative Adults

Here are some ways that training children in creative thinking can help them as imaginative grown-ups.

First, they are more likely to listen to God's voice. Creative adults who have learned to think clearly and are open to fresh or unusual ideas will also be open to the Holy Spirit's leading. Chances are that they will refuse to conform to ungodly thinking and will have the courage to voice unpopular ideas that others might be too timid to advance.

Next, training in creative thinking will contribute to your child's career success. Adults who know how to think creatively are a jump ahead of their competition. They recognize their creative flash, and they will work until they have a useful product.

Finally, they will set a good example for their children by listening and responding sensitively to their ideas. Believe it. If you are a good model for your kids, there is an excellent chance they will follow in your footsteps. Don't expect a carbon copy, but experience shows that children turn out to be about the same kind of adult as their mom or dad.

Overcoming a Handicap

Even without a parent's good example, ordinary-acting children have overcome difficult, imperfect childhoods to become highly creative adults. By surmounting serious obstacles children have turned a bad situation into a creative one, conquering poor teaching, physical handicaps, or poor emotional adjustment. Here are a few stories about the childhood of famous adults.

1. Charles Shultz, creator of the characters in the *Peanuts* comic strip was never allowed to draw cartoons in school. "Only in the seventh grade one time. . . . The teacher for one brief period let us experiment with drawing political cartoons. . . . Outside of that I don't recall ever being allowed to draw cartoons."[1]

2. The following story about young James Watts can't be documented, but it makes interesting reading. In 1784, when James was twelve years old, he was scolded by his aunt for watching a kettle boil. "Are you not ashamed spending your time in this way?" he was asked. The story goes on to tell how this Scottish schoolboy's fascination with steam later led to the invention of the steam engine.[2]

3. As a child Robert Louis Stevenson was tormented by nightmares that caused him to wake up screaming. Stevenson later described how his dreams "Became a stage upon which he conceived some of his best stories."[3]

4. If Buckminister Fuller's teacher hadn't been sensitive to his talent he might not have become a creative genius. At first glance perhaps no kindergarten child appeared less inventive than Buckminister Fuller. He was farsighted and cross-eyed and unable to see many of the sights other children enjoyed. He describes the day in 1899 that his invention, the geodesic dome, had its beginnings.

> One of my first days at kindergarten the teacher brought us some toothpicks and semidried peas and told us to make structures. The other children, who had good eyes, were familiar with houses and barns; with my bad sight, I was used to seeing only bulks—I had no feeling at all about structural lines. Because I couldn't see, I naturally had recourse to my other senses which were very sensitive. When the teacher told me to make structures, I tried to make something that would work.
>
> Pushing and pulling, I found that a triangle held its shape when nothing else did. The other children made rectangular structures that seemed to stand up because the peas held them in shape. Meanwhile, after pushing and pulling, the triangle I made felt good.
>
> The teacher called all the other teachers in the primary school as well as the kindergarten to look at this triangular structure. I remember being surprised that they were surprised. I began to feel then that all nature's structuring and patterning must be based on triangles.[4]

Years later Fuller used the triangle as the basic shape of the dome. In the late 1950s the "dome boom" began, and his domes were in demand around the world. We can't be certain, but perhaps the encouragement of Bucky's kindergarten teacher helped him to continue thinking about the triangle.

Do Smart Kids Become Creative Adults?

The work of people like Schultz, Stevenson, Watts, and Fuller illustrates another element of creativity that needs to be considered. That is, superior intelligence is necessary for highly creative works, but the smart person is not always creative. What this means is that a certain amount of intelligence is required for creativity. Beyond that, being more or less intelligent doesn't always determine the level of a child or adult's creativity.

Children who learn to be creative thinkers have the potential to be creative adults, but the puzzle is that some reach that potential and some don't. In fact, even gifted children with high IQs who are placed in special classes for smart kids aren't guaranteed that they will be creative adults.

The results of research by Lewis M. Terman, professor of psychology at Stanford University, seem to show that gifted children may not grow up to be creative adults. Terman was a pioneer in intelligence testing and is the developer of the respected Stanford-Binet Intelligence Test.

In 1921 Terman launched a long-range study of approximately fifteen hundred California boys and girls who were seven to fifteen years old. These weren't ordinary kids. They were extremely bright children who scored above the ninety-ninth percentile on the Stanford-Binet Intelligence Test. By gathering information periodically about each child, he was able to follow these children into adulthood. The results of the study show that high IQ children are superior to average children in physique, health, social adjustment, and school achievement. Most entered the professions as adults.[5]

But what about their creativity? In 1985 Doris Wallace wrote that the "1000 high IQ children selected in 1925, who are well past middle age, have not produced a single truly illustrious individual."[6]

Common Creative Traits

Where does that leave us? I think it means that creative children can become creative adults, but if left to their own resources, even very smart kids won't always grow up to be creative. There are at least four traits that creative children and adults share. If parents reinforce these traits in their children, they will probably carry over to maturity. These influential traits are:

1. *Curiosity.*—All creative individuals are curious. It is a trait that can't be ignored by parents who want their children to become creative adults. You can begin encouraging creativity when your child is an infant. Babies show their curiosity when they touch, grab, feel, and stuff their mouths with anything they can reach. Children a little older love to walk outside and brush leaves with their fingers, point to birds, pinch the grass, and babble about what they see.

2. *Persistence.*—This trait is essential to the creative adult. Children learn to be persistent when they move ahead after failure. The track record of creative adults shows they experience one failure after another, but in spite of the flops, they endure until their creative idea unfolds as a useful product.

3. *Positive self-esteem.*—What parents say to their children, how well they listen, and the way they discipline them affects self-esteem. If kids are convinced they can't think, the feeling hovers over them to maturity. Creative thinking cannot soar in that kind of environment.

4. *Openness.*—This trait ties together the other traits of the creative personality. Openness is an attitude that if cultivated will serve the creative person as a child or adult. Marshall Cook writes about the creative personality in his book *Freeing Your Creativity*. He believes that the creative personality displays:

- an openness to experience,
- an openness to possibilities,
- an open mind about ways to go about solving a problem,
- and most of all, instead of walls closing us off, an open door to pass through in discovering new abilities, new interests, new powers.[7]

Putting It Together

Growing creative kids isn't easy, but the traits of curiosity, persistence, openness, and self-esteem are the mix that helps kids develop their creative potential.

Little and Scott's list of ten characteristics of well-adjusted children can serve as a guide for helping children reach their creative potential. These characteristics are crucial and ones that Christian parents can subscribe to. Come back to them occasionally and check on your child's progress. You might even make a copy of the list and tack it up where it's easy to see.

Ten Wishes for My Child

1. To respect the rights of others.
2. To be tolerant of others.
3. To cooperate with others.
4. To encourage others.
5. To be courageous.
6. To have a true sense of her own worth.
7. To feel he belongs.
8. To have socially acceptable goals.
9. To put forth genuine effort.
10. To be willing to share rather than think "how much can I get."[8]

Points to Remember

1. Children who learn creative thinking skills have a good chance of remembering and using those skills as adults.

2. Creative children can overcome obstacles and become creative adults.

3. Research shows that not all smart kids are creative kids.

4. There were no Nobel laureates in Terman's long-range study of 1,500 gifted individuals.

5. Curiosity is one of the most important traits shared by creative children and adults.

6. The truly creative adult will find a way to fill a need. Many simple ideas have blessed us.

7. Poor self-esteem is hard to defeat. It often sticks with a child into adulthood.

Family Activities

1. Find autobiographies and biographies of creative individuals and read them with your child. Talk about the events in the person's childhood.

2. Invite interesting people to your home. Let the kids sit in on the discussions, make comments, and ask questions.

3. When your child develops a strong interest in a topic, try to find an adult willing to be her mentor.

4. Ask your child's teacher to sponsor a series on creativity, and ask guests to talk about their work. The series could include creative children and adults. For example, an author of children's books might spend part of a day with the class talking about how he started writing and his experiences as a writer. Later, several children might tell about their writing and read samples to the class.

Notes

1. Marilee Zendek, *The Right Side of the Brain* (New York: McGraw-Hill, 1983), 56.

2. Ann Elwood and Carol Orsag Madigan, *Brainstorms and Thunderbolts* (New York: Macmillan, 1983).

3. Ibid., 273.

4. Ibid., 31-34.

5. Leslie Dorman and Peter Edidin, "Original Spin," *Psychology Today,* July/August 1989.

6. Doris B. Wallace, "Giftedness and the Construction of a Creative Life," in *The Gifted and Talented Developmental Perspectives* (American Psychological Association: Washington, 1985), 362.

7. Marshall Cook, *Freeing Your Creativity* (Cincinnati: Writer's Digest Books, 1992), 37.

8. Mary Little and Mary Scott, "Parenting: Helping Gifted-Talented-Creative Children Reach Their Potential," *The Creative Child and Adult Quarterly,* 14 (1990): 146.

PART III:

Your Family's Plan

11

Fourteen Creative Thinking Workouts

These fourteen creative thinking workouts are an exercise program to help develop your child's creative thinking abilities. Most children understand that athletes warm up, and stretch their muscles before they begin a workout or competition. Then comes the strenuous workout, followed by a time to cool down, and a time to enjoy the rush of accomplishment.

Children should have the same experience with their creative thinking workout. The warm-up exercises start the process, and the workout challenges their thinking. The cool down leaves the child with a feeling of accomplishment and prepares the child for the transition to other activities.[1]

Make the whole workout something your child looks forward to. The warm-up and cool down take only a few minutes, and they reinforce the main workout activity. Have the brainstorming rules and Discovery Checklist (pp. 40-41) available for each workout, since they introduce important principles of problem solving.

When your child has completed the fourteen lessons, you can make your own plans using the "Creative Thinking Planner" or a format you devise to fit your family.

Family Meetings

The type of family meeting you select depends on family members' schedules and the age of your children. Since creativity develops best in a loosely structured and spontaneous atmosphere, try to keep your child's interest level high by planning activities ahead of time.

Psychologists Don Dinkmeyer and Gary McKay have developed a systematic approach to parent-child relations. Here are several of their guidelines for planning and carrying out successful family meetings:

1. *Hold regular meetings.*—Once you have decided how, when, and how often your family will meet, keep to the schedule. Set a time limit so the meeting won't become tedious. Plan a variety of activities to keep the meeting lively. Twenty to thirty minutes is the maximum.

2. *Keep a record.*—If brainstorming is one of the activities, record the decisions and try to decide on the best solution. Reaching a concensus is less competitive than voting. Dinkmeyer says that younger children may feel their vote isn't as important as the vote of older brothers or sisters, and losers may oppose the decision of other family members.

3. *Be clear on your goals.*—Don't be tempted to use the meeting to distribute jobs or discipline your kids. It also isn't a gripe session. Save these subjects for another time and another type of family meeting.

4. *Recognize creative ideas and accomplishments.*— Provide time to acknowledge the creative things that are happening in your family. Let your children read their stories or act out plays they have written. Display their art work.

5. *End on a positive note.*—Save time for recreation by taking a few minutes to play your family's favorite game.

If family members object to the meetings, try a less formal route. You can plan your creative development program and slip in the activities at odd times during the day. Have crayons, colored marking pens, and other art materials ready before your child asks to work on an art project. When you are sitting around talking, start brainstorming by asked a "What if . . . ?" question.

Finally, there are some common mistakes that parents

make in their family meetings. Here are tips to help you keep your meetings on track:

- Don't start late.
- Don't let the meeting run too long.
- Don't dominate the meeting.
- Don't permit complaints or criticisms.
- Don't be too serious. Remember to have fun.[2]

Use the Creative Thinking Planner to help you develop your family's creative workouts.

Creative Thinking Planner

Week number ____
Our objectives are:
    Use lesson number ____
    Make a new plan   ____
    Other   ____

Activities:

Brainstorming	____	Imagination development	____
PMI	____	Humor and riddles	____
Forced relationships	____	Quantity of ideas	____
Attribute listing	____	Original ideas	____
Review	____	Flexible thinking	____
		Other	____

Materials:

Art paper	____	Brainstorming Rules Chart	____
Crayons, paints etc.	____	Discovery Checklist	____
Writing paper	____	Other	____

Evaluation:
    Did the lesson go as planned? ____
    Were the objectives achieved? ____

Creative Workout 1: Problem Solving

Objectives

Learn to be sensitive to problems.

Practice problem solving using the PMI (Plus, Minus, Interesting Problem Solver).

Props

A small chalkboard or notebook

A scrapbook for drawings and magazine cutouts.

Activity Description

The preschool activity develops imagination. It is suited for preschool and early elementary school-age children, but older children may enjoy participating, too.

The elementary-age activity helps children practice asking key questions before brainstorming a problem. This strengthens children's creative problem solving abilities.

There are two questions that help define a problem and set the stage for a creative solution. The first is "What do I want to find out?" And the second is "How can I make the problem clearer?"

Actions

Preschool Warm-up

Look through newspapers and magazines for pictures of different kinds of balloons, for example, hot-air balloons, party balloons, multicolored balloons, and tiny balloons. Cut the pictures out and glue them to a piece of notebook paper. Talk about the characteristics of each balloon.

Preschool Workout

Stretch out on the floor with your child, get comfortable, and imagine you are balloons. Slowly fill with air. How does it feel to puff up and sail away? . . . Go up and bump the ceiling. . . . Slowly float down. . . . Watch out for the nail on the wall. . . . Ouch! Did it hurt when the nail stuck you? . . . I'm leaking air. Are you? . . . Let's float gently to the floor. . . . Let all of your air out and relax. . . . Would you like to be a balloon again?

Preschool Cool Down

Let your child choose his favorite balloon picture for an Imagination Scrapbook.

Early and Late Elementary Warm-up

Take a few minutes to sit with your child and talk about any problems he has, for example, problems with friends, school, rules, or household chores. Jot down the problems he mentions. Then choose two or three for a brainstorming session.

Choose a familiar kitchen object like a mechanical or electric can opener. Ask your child to invent new uses for the item. Limit the time to no longer than five minutes. If your kid gets stuck, encourage him to mentally take the opener apart and reassemble it to make another object.

Early and Late Elementary Workout

Restate the problems using as guides the questions, "What do I want to find out?" and "How can I make the problem clearer?" Write the revised problems in a notebook or a small chalkboard.

Choose one of the problems to solve using the PMI (Plus, Minus, Interesting) format. If you need to review the PMI, check chapter 1, pages 12 and 18. Set a time limit, and don't forget to record the problem-solving ideas. With young children, mom or dad will need to do the recording. Don't hold back, but get the ideas out as rapidly as possible. Also, remember to wait until later to evaluate ideas.

When the PMI is completed choose the solutions that are the best for your family.

Problem: (State in one sentence)_____

_____ .

	Check		
	Plus	*Minus*	*Interesting*
Ideas			
1.			
2.			
3.			

Early and late Elementary Cool Down

Invent a machine to weigh a hippopotamus.

This game can be played individually or team against team. Each person or team is instructed to invent a machine that will weigh a hippo. Give the following directions to the game players.
  1. Use paper and pencil to sketch your invention.
  2. When you have an idea how the invention will look, paste together parts of magazine pictures to illustrate it.
  3. Design a Super Inventor Certificate for the players.

Creative Workout 2: Brainstorming

Objectives
  Introduce the brainstorming rules.
  Practice brainstorming.

Props
  Make a chart of the brainstorming rules, and tape it to the wall or on a door where it can easily be seen. Refer to chapter 3 for a refresher on brainstorming.
  The rules are:
  1. Free your imagination.
  2. The more ideas the better.
  3. Combine your ideas to make better ones.
  4. Wait to judge the ideas.

Activity Description
  Brainstorming is an activity that preschool and school age children can enjoy. Kent Burtt, author of *Smart Times,* says, "Even little kids can learn to brainstorm if you pose hypothetical problems that interest them. . . . Ask a question—not a yes/no, right/wrong kind of question but an open-ended one. Then you, your child, and perhaps your spouse, too, can generate answers."[3]

Actions
Preschool Warm-up
  Ask your child to "Think of as many uses as you can for

a bed." Allow two or three minutes for answers. If your child is reluctant to try, it's OK to help. Make it a fun few minutes.

Preschool Workout

Try these brainstorming questions for young children.

Say "Think of as many uses as you can for a toothbrush, a sand bucket, or a colored pencil."

Ask "What would happen if we bought ten birds and ten cats?" "What would happen if you were a tiny rabbit?"

Concentrate on the first brainstorming rule, and don't worry if the ideas aren't practical.

Preschool Cool Down

Help your preschooler create the world's strangest animal by cutting up animal pictures and gluing head, legs, tails, ears, and other parts together to make an outlandish animal.

Early and Late Elementary Warm-up

Try these brainstorming problems. Ask the kids to use their imaginations to produce a quantity of ideas. Explain that no idea is too crazy to express. Remember to encourage fluency of ideas.

Say "Think of as many ideas as you can for unusual uses of . . . ."

- An old TV set
- A broken skateboard

Early and Late Elementary Workout

Plan a meal around a theme your child suggests. For example, choosing table decorations and menu items that reflect her favorite color or hobby would be one way to start. Try to think of a large number of ideas that would fit the theme.

Build new ideas by combining two other ideas. Does it make a better idea? Encourage mind stretching and wild speculation. For the time being forget about logic and get a little crazy.

Decide how each family member will help out. Start making the table decorations

Early and Late Elementary Cool Down
   Create the world's strangest animal.—This is a combination game and art project. It can be played as a team game or by individuals. The game can be played anytime, but may come in handy when the kids say "there is nothing to do."
   Provide each team with a pair of scissors, paste or white glue, large pieces of colored poster paper for background, and a supply of old magazines. Each team creates a new, strange animal. If there aren't enough players for teams, each person can make his or her creation. Display the pictures in a prominent place.

Creative Workout 3: Brainstorming

Objectives
   Practice using the Discovery Checklist.
   Review the brainstorming rules.
   Practice imagination development.

Props
   The Discovery Checklist.—This checklist (p. 41) helps children change and improve their ideas and think of new ones. It also stimulates children to think in unconventional ways.

   Brainstorming chart.—Highlight the second brainstorming rule (the more ideas the better). This rule encourages children to express all their ideas, including the absurd ones.

Activity Description
   The goal of this activity is to produce a large quantity of ideas; don't worry if your child's ideas seem off-the-wall or absurd. When the time comes to evaluate ideas, it is easy to tone them down or build on the zany ones.
   Show your child the two charts, and go over the questions on each list. Explain that the questions and rules on the charts will help her think of new ideas.

Actions
Warm-up (All Ages)

The following warm-up exercise may be used for pre-school or elementary grade children.

Choose a mystery item. Anything that is unfamiliar to your child will do. A hand-operated coffee grinder, a razor-blade sharpener, or a meat slicer are perfect. Ask your child to think of as many uses as she can for the mystery object. When she has named all the possible uses, explain how it is used.

Preschool and Early Elementary Workout

Help your child stretch her imagination by wondering about things that might happen. To begin the activity, ask what she wonders about? Make a list of your child's remarks.

Turn each remark into the question "I wonder what would happen if . . . ?

If the activity drags ask "I wonder what would happen if you stayed awake all night?"

Continue by making up other "What if . . . ?" questions.

Late Elementary Workout

Start with the question "What would happen if dinosaurs came back to earth?"

Say "What would happen if everyone in the word used sign language instead of speech?"

Make a game of wondering, and help your child make up similar questions. Write the ideas in a notebook, and choose the best ones when the workout is finished.

Cool Down (All ages)

Say "Can you imagine a sea creature with two pairs of hands? How would it use its hands?"

If your preschooler or early elementary child doesn't know what a sea creature is, switch to something familiar.

Make a list of all the things the creature can do. Ask your child to draw a sketch of the sea creature and name it.

Imagineering
Play the imagineering game, "The Aquarium," found in the appendix.

Creative Workout 4: Problem-Solving Questions

Objectives
Learn to ask questions that help solve problems.
Practice imagination development.

Props
The Brainstorming Rules Chart and Discovery Checklist.
A small chalkboard or notebook.

Activity Description
Creative children tend to look at problems differently than less creative children. They know how to discover the facts of a problem and how to use the facts to solve the problem. This activity teaches your child to look at the facts of a problem, think of ways to solve it, and decide on the best solution.

Actions
Preschool Warm-up
Read your preschool youngster a favorite animal story. For instance, Beatrix Potter's *Peter Rabbit* is a timeless tale loved by children.

Preschool Workout
Help your child make up a story about a pet rabbit, a kitten, a puppy, or other animal. Find out the facts about the make-believe pet. What is its name, size, and color? Is it male or female? Where does it live? How old is it?
Next, introduce a problem into the story. What if the pet is lost? Help your child think of all the places a lost pet might be. Decide on the best way to find the animal.

Early and Late Elementary Warm-up
Choose one of your child's favorite stores and search for the facts of the story. Ask about the main character's prob-

lem. What did the hero do to solve the problem? Think of other ways to solve it. Ask your child what she would do to help solve the problem.

Early and Late Elementary Workout

Read the following scenario to your child: Arthur's bad day started on the school bus. In the first five minutes he punched Bobby in the stomach and spit at him. When the bus driver told him to sit down, he walked by Bobby's seat, grabbed his lunch, and threw it to the end of the bus. The bus driver reported Arthur to the principal, and she called Arthur's parents.

Talk with your child about the events on the bus. Then ask: "What have you learned about Arthur's bus trip?" List the facts your youngster mentions.

Ask "What else would you like to know?" And "How could you get this information?"

Ask "How can you help Arthur behave better on the school bus?" Encourage your child to stretch her thinking to produce original ideas.

Cool Down (All Ages)

Choose a Bible story and retell it from the perspective of one of the characters, but not the main character. For example, the story of "Jonah and the Whale" can be told from the outlook of the whale.

If it's an unfamiliar story, read it first, then retell the story. Or let older children rewrite it from a different character's viewpoint.

Imagineering Game

Play the imagineering game, "When Moses was a Baby," found in the appendix.

Creative Workout 5: Producing Ideas

Objectives

Review problem-solving strategies.
Practice imagination development.

Props
   The Discovery Checklist.
   A notebook or tape recorder to record ideas.

Activity Description
   Children can learn new ways to change and improve their ideas, and this workout will teach your child to produce a variety of ideas in a short period. Remember not to evaluate ideas until the activity is completed.

Actions
Preschool Warm-up
   Tune up your child's creative thinking with the following questions.
   Say "Imagine what would happen if snails were fast and rabbits were slow?" or "What if we walked as slowly as turtles?"

Preschool Workout
   Ask "How can you make your doll (toy truck, tricycle, etc.) better?"
   Ask "What can you change?" "What can you add?" "What can you take away?"
   Use the Discovery Checklist to help your child think of ways to improve each item. Three or four minutes should be enough for this activity.

Preschool Cool Down
   Draw a picture to show how snails would look if they ran like rabbits.

Early and Late Elementary Warm-Up
   Say "Imagine what would happen if kids were astronauts or children lived on a space station?"

Early and Late Elementary Exercises
   Continue the questioning used in the preschooler's workout, but increase the difficulty of the questions. Follow the Discovery Checklist questions. Start by asking "What can you do to make your room nicer?

Ask your child to read a story and try to think of ways it can be improved. For example, what can you add to the plot? Can a character be changed to make the story better?

Early and Late Elementary Cool Down
Ask your child to "Design a space station for kids."

Imagineering Game
Play the imagineering game, "Boxes," found in the appendix.

Creative Workout 6: Forming New Ideas

Objectives
Practice creating ideas.
Learn to change ideas by improving them.

Props
Writing materials or a tape recorder.
The Discovery Checklist.
White or colored paper, crayons, felt-tip pens.

Activity Description
The first activity is designed to help children think of a large number of ideas in a short time. Encourage a rapid-fire pace. Remember, the more ideas the better. Allow three to five minutes for each activity. When the time is up count the ideas.

The second activity, flip-flops, is fun for all age levels and encourages children to stretch their imagination for new ideas.

Action
Preschool Warm-up
Emphasize that you want your child to think of as many answers to your questions as she can. Don't ask questions that can be answered yes or no. Here are a few to try.
Say: "Tell me everything that tastes sour."
Ask: "How many boys or girls names can you think of?"

Preschool Workout

Try these "flip-flops." Ask your child to imagine what would happen if . . .

- fish flew and birds swam?
- cats sang and birds meowed?
- dogs hopped and rabbits barked?

Make up several of your own flip-flops.

Early and Late Elementary Warm-up

Show a familiar object to your child and ask him to think of unusual uses for it. Ideas for a toothbrush might be "a hamster's hairbrush, a flag pole, a brush to wash toys."

Early and Late Elementary Workout

Try these flip-flops with older children. Ask your child to imagine what would happen if . . .

- Lions squeaked and mice roared?
- Elephants were as playful as kittens?
- Ice cream was as sour as pickles?

Cool Down (All Ages)

Help your child make up a flip-flop and tell a story using it as the story plot. (On Monday the lion woke up at dawn, stretched until his body felt loose and comfortable, and roared. But instead of his feared roar, he squeaked like a mouse.)

Imagineering Game

Play the imagineering game, "The Circus," found in the appendix.

Creative Workout 7: Forced Relationships

Objectives

Learn about forced relationships.

Learn to substitute one idea for another.

Learn to make up riddles.

Props
 Discovery Checklist
 Brainstorming rules

Activity Description
 Forced relationships requires children to think of a connection between two unrelated objects or ideas. It's OK to encourage outlandish thinking.

Actions
Preschool Warm-up
 Begin with some simple riddles. Preschoolers enjoy riddles even if they miss the punchline, and riddles increase your child's sense of fun with words. How does your child respond to this traditional English riddle?

> As light as a feather,
> As round as a ball
> Yet all the king's men
> Cannot carry it at all.
> What is it? (Answer: A bubble.)[4]

Preschool Creative Thinking Exercises
 Before beginning to practice forced relationships, display items or show pictures of the items you want to use in the workout. Let your child look at each object before you ask how the objects are connected. When your child has given all the answers you think are forthcoming, try another relationship. Here are a few to try:
 1. Ask your child "How are crayons and bicycles alike?" (Kids use them, they're fun.)
 2. "How are peppermint candy and strawberry jam alike?"
 3. "How are ladders and stairs alike?"
 A riddle is a good followup to this activity. Susan Amerikaner suggests parents help their children combine "some of the characteristics of an object to make a riddle." She says a riddle for a ladder or stairs might be "What goes up and down, but stays in the same place?"[5]

Early and Late Elementary Warm-up
Talk to your child about riddles and let him ask you his favorite one.

If the activity bogs down, ask the old standby: "What's black and white and red (read) all over?" (Answer: a newspaper.)

Early and Late Elementary Workout
For early elementary school children, the relationship between two items can be presented as a two-part problem. First, the parent asks how the two objects are alike, followed by the question, How can one object be improved by being more like the other?

Write your child's answers on a sheet of paper and refer to them later. Here are two examples:

1. How are a book and a newspaper alike? How can a book be improved by making it more like a newspaper?

2. How are a desk and a chair alike? How can a desk and chair be improved by combining them?

More difficult concepts and relationships can be explored by older elementary children. For instance, choose three similar objects. Ask your child to explain how they are the same and how they are different. Be sure to take time to evaluate the ideas.

Ask your child to invent a new product by combining three objects. Finally, encourage him to draw a picture or make a model of his invention—explaining how it works.

Cool Down (All Ages)
Tell knock-knock riddles. Here is an ageless one.
Knock, knock.
Who's there?
Boo.
Boo who?
Don't cry, baby, that's all right.

Creative Workout 8: Forced Relationships

Objectives

Practice finding original ideas.

Practice brainstorming.

Props

An assortment of children's toys.

Kitchen articles: bottle, spatula, eggbeater, plastic bowl, tongs, and so on.

Activity Description

This workout helps children see the link in unrelated items. Because some children have difficulty thinking imaginatively, praise your child's attempts at original thinking. Encourage building on the ideas of other family members, but don't evaluate the ideas until the end of the workout.

Actions

Preschool Warm-up

Show your child each of the kitchen utensils you have selected. Ask the following questions:

"What is this?"

"What is it called?"

"What can you do with it?"

"How do I use it when I am cooking?"

Preschool Workout

Choose a few of your child's toys and place two of them on a table. Ask your child to think of ways the toys can be combined to make a new toy or a new game. Help her think of a name for each new items.

Preschool Cool Down

Play a guessing game. Say "Close your eyes. I will make an animal sound and you guess the name of the animal." Try a snake (sss-ssss-sssss!) or an owl (whoo-oooo-oooo!).

Ask "How would it sound if a snake and an owl were singing together?"

Reverse the questioning and let your preschooler make the animal noises and you do the guessing.

Early and Late Elementary Warm-up
Ask your child to tell "How a footprint is like a map, a horse is like a car, a baby is like a flower."[6]

Early and Late Elementary Workout
Choose several things from around the house, like tools, bottles, toys, or other everyday household articles. Ask your child to choose three of the objects and place them in a row.

Ask "Which one could be improved by combining it with something else?"

Together, select the best combinations and talk about the reasons for selecting them.

Review the brainstorming rules and then say: "Suppose your three-year-old sister threw a temper tantrum when things didn't go her way. One day your mother left you in charge until she returned from shopping. While you were playing together your sister screamed, cried, and kicked the wall because she couldn't play with your toy. What would you do?" Think of ways you could solve this problem.

Early and Late Elementary Cool Down
Present the following problem to your child, but hold off brainstorming for a few days.

Say: "I'm going to give you a problem to think about. Some boys and girls can't get along with the kids at school, and no one likes them. How can you help other children like these boys and girls?"

Imagineering Game
Play the imagineering game, "The World's Strangest Automobile," found in the appendix.

Creative Workout 9: Forced Relationships
Objectives
Use forced relationships to solve problems.

Props
Notebook paper to record your child's ideas.
Discovery Checklist.

Activity Description
Forced relationships teaches children to expand their creative thinking. Professor Sidney Parnes gives the following example:
A family was trying to think of ways to make their meals more enjoyable. They decided to look out the window for ideas. One child spotted the maple tree's leaves and suggested decorating the table with them. Another child thought of carving table decorations from the tree bark. They listened to the birds chirping and thought it would be nice to have music while they ate. In this way the family used their imagination to solve a family dilemma.[7]

Actions
Warm-up (all ages)
For a warm-up, ask your child to think of as many ways as possible to decorate a room, table, or wall.

Workout (all ages)
Follow the warm-up by using forced relationships to solve a simple problem. Look at a tree (grass, sky, flowers, etc.). Ask "How could we use some part of the tree to decorate the kitchen?" Record the ideas, and you and your child choose the best two or three. Try out the decorating ideas.
Continue by planning a dinner menu around what your child sees through the window. Ask "Does the tree help you think of anything for the menu?"
Use the same question for a bird, flowers, leaf, sky. Write down each menu item and when the flow of ideas has ebbed choose the final menu for your meal.

Preschool Cool Down
Suggest that your child make up a game and teach it to the rest of the family. Be sure you get the directions and rules in writing.

Early and Late Elementary Cool Down

Refer to the Workout 8, for early and late elementary cool down children.

Say "Remember the problem I gave you to think about?"

Repeat the problem: "Some boys and girls can't get along with the other kids at school, and no one likes them. How can you help other children to like these boys and girls?"

Creative Workout 10: Attribute Listing

Objectives

List and improve the attributes of an object.

Encourage children to think imaginatively.

Props

Discovery Checklist

Notebook and pencil

Mystery Box: include an assortment of familiar objects

Activity Description

Attribute listing examines an object, then helps the child discover ways to improve it. In this workout children are asked to list an object's attributes or characteristics and to think of ways to improve each attribute.

Discuss with your child the meaning of an attribute and use the Discovery Checklist to think of ways to improve each trait.

Actions

Warm-up (all ages)

Fill a cardboard box with an assortment of odds and ends. Include a variety of familiar and not so familiar objects, including toys, tools, utensils, and so on. You also need a cloth blindfold or mask to cover the player's eyes.

The players take turns putting on the blindfold and removing an object from the box. After making a selection, each player removes the blindfold and tells everything he knows about the object.

Younger children may need their parent's help, and it's OK to give hints about the object. Use a kitchen timer to signal the end of each player's turn. Start with a time limit of one or two minutes.

Preschool Workout

Choose several objects for attribute listing. It's not necessary, however, to limit the workout to articles in the Mystery Box. Tailor the kinds of objects you choose to the interests of your child.

Say "Think of all the ways to use . . . (the object chosen). Examples are a storybook, a toy telephone, a tricycle, building blocks, and so on).

Make a list of the attributes and help your child evaluate his responses.

Early and Late Elementary Workout

The activity for early elementary kids is the same as for preschool children, except for an additional question. After you have listed the attributes, ask your child to think of ways to improve each attribute.

For example, first ask "How many different ways can you use a . . . ?" Follow this question by saying, "Think of all the way you can improve a . . . ."

Use the following items for practice: a wristwatch, a computer, a paperback book. Also, choose objects from the Mystery Box.

Ask your child to think of all the attributes of an honest person and someone who is fair. Combine these attributes by asking "how are honesty and fairness are alike?"

Try listing the attributes of other values, and discuss the ideas and values with your child.

Cool Down (All ages)

Play the imagineering game, "Happy Birthday," found in the appendix.

Lesson 11: Attribute Listing

Objectives
   Produce new ideas through attribute listing.
   Improve imaginative thinking.

Props
   Discovery Checklist.
   Crayons, colored pencils, colored marker pens, drawing paper.

Activity Description
   First, ask your child to list the attributes of two objects. Next, ask her to explain how the two items are alike. As in other lessons, encourage children to stretch their imaginations and wait to evaluate their ideas. Remember to keep the session fun and lively.
   The cool down exercise is an imagineering game, suitable for all age levels. Players answer the questions silently, but the answers can be shared at the end of the game.

Actions
Preschool Warm-up
   Set several objects in a row on a small table, for instance, a kitchen spoon, a drinking glass, a bowl, and a pencil. Ask your child to think of ways to use each item.

Preschool Workout
   Following the warm-up, show an unfamiliar object, like a flour sifter, a potato masher, or a rolling pin. Ask your child to think of as many uses as possible for the object. Afterwards, explain what it is, and show how it works.

Preschool Cool down
   Play the imagineering game at the end of the Creative Workout.

Early and Late Elementary Warm-up
   Display a flashlight or other object you have selected.
   Say "A flashlight is a useful tool. Tell me all the different uses of a flashlight."

Say "What else can be used as a flashlight? How is it different?"

Say "Combine them to make something new." What would it look like?"

Say "Give your invention a name and draw a picture of it."

Elementary Workout

Make a list of unusual inventions. An egg cooker, flip-up sunglasses, a reading light that attaches to a book are a few unique inventions. Ask your child to explain how these inventions help other people.

Next, ask your child to think of absurd inventions for children. For a starter, say "What about inventing something that will help kids pick up their dirty clothes? Do their homework? Do housework?"

After several inventions have been mentioned, say "Write a description of your best idea and illustrate it."

Cool Down (all ages)

Imagineering Game.—Say "Pretend you are covered with soft, silky fur, and can change your color and shape. What are you? What do you look like?

"Now you are bright blue. If you don't like that color change to one you like. Now what do you look like?

"You are the largest soft and furry thing in the world. How big are you? What would happen if you became so small no one could see you?

"Now slowly begin to change into your real self. How does it feel to be back?"

Lesson 12: Attribute Listing

Objectives

Practice attribute listing.
Practice brainstorming.

Props

Discovery Checklist and Brainstorming Rules Chart.
Paper, pencils, crayons, or colored marking pens.

Magazine pictures, toys, stuffed animals, and other objects familiar to your child.

Activity Description

This workout continues to develop the use of attribute listing. Make sure your child understands the meaning of an attribute.

Actions

Preschool Warm-up

Find pictures of a cat, dog, fish, bird, candle, light bulb, ice-cream cone, and candy bar. Begin by holding up the pictures of a dog and cat, and ask your preschooler:

"How is a cat like a dog?" If answers come slowly, it's OK to name some attributes. Your goal is a large number of ideas in a short period. Talk about the characteristics of each animal or item.

Preschool Workout

Continue asking questions like "How is a . . .

- "fish like a bird?
- "candle like a light bulb?
- "candy bar like an ice-cream cone?"

How many fresh ideas did your child think of?

Preschool Cool Down

Talk about zoo animals for a few minutes. Browse through an animal picture book and discuss their likenesses and differences.

Early and Late Elementary Warm-up

Give your child a blank piece of paper and a pencil and ask him to answer the following questions. He may choose to write the answers or give them orally.

"How is a tape recorder like a video recorder?"

"How is a station wagon like a kangaroo?"

If only a few answers are given, ask "Are they alike in some other way? Think of all the ways they are alike."

Early and Late Elementary Workout

Use the Brainstorming Rules Chart to review the four rules. During this activity stress the third brainstorming rule—learning to build on other ideas.

Record your child's ideas, and after five minutes check the number of ideas recorded and evaluate them. Is he learning to build on the ideas of others and to use original thinking?

Say "What would happen if water animals could live on land and land animals could live in the water?"

Early and Late Elementary Cool down

Build phrases using the same beginning letter, for example, An Apple Appears, Buy Buttered Bread, Collect Canceled Checks.

See how many letters of the alphabet your child uses before he is stumped.

Creative Workout 13: Problem Solving

Objectives

Review creative problem solving

Learn to analyze a problem.

Props

The Discovery Checklist

Activity Description

This exercise teaches three necessary questions for creative problem solving.

• *Fact-finding questions.*—These questions allow children to get the background information they need for solving a problem. For older children, this first set of questions may mean spending time at the library, reading, and gathering information.

• *Idea-finding questions.*—The Discovery Checklist aids in asking these questions and can be used with the "Plus," "Minus," and "Interesting," (PMI) problem-solving questions.

• *Solution-finding questions.*—At this stage the goal is to find the best solution for the problem. To evaluate the best solution list all of the "plus," "minus," and "interesting" ideas. Finally, use these lists to decide if the solution is a good one.

Actions
Preschool Warm-up
Take time to sit and wonder with your child. This is an excellent time to talk about the wonder of God's love and care for children.

Preschool Workout
Start with the following question: "I wonder what would happen if . . . We moved to new home? I couldn't go to school? My friend wouldn't let me play with her?"
After a few minutes, try some of your own questions. Include farfetched ideas and see how many practical solutions result. Talk about facts and solutions.

Preschool Cool Down
Make up a story and take turns adding ideas to the plot, for example:
Parent: One day Jesus was walking and saw . . .
Child: Two kids playing . . .
Parent: Jesus smiled and said . . .
Child: "Come and talk to me."

Early and Late Elementary Warm-up
Say "Suppose you weren't allowed to sing. What would happen if it was against the law to sing?"

Early and Late Elementary Workout
Ask a family member to read the following story:
Julie went to a baseball game with her family. Her mom said it would be OK to take her friend, Sara, if they watched the game and didn't act up. Before the girls went

into the ball park Julie's dad said, "If you want to leave your seats, tell me first." Both girls agreed.

In the middle of the seventh inning Julie looked around, jumped up, and raced up the aisle. Nearly twenty minutes passed before she returned. Her dad was furious.

"I thought I told you not to leave your seat unless you told me where you were going," he said. Julie looked away without answering him.

Ask your child to answer the following questions:

"What happened in this story?"

"What facts do you need to know?"

"Think of ways to solve this problem."

Place your kid's solutions in plus, minus, and interesting (PMI) categories. Finally, use these lists to decide on the best way to solve the problem.

Early and Late Elementary Cool Down

Ask your child to think of a problem that hasn't been solved. Apply the three kinds of questions to the problem, and see what kind of solution evolves.

Play the imagineering game, "A Trip to Jerusalem," found in the appendix.

Creative Workout 14: Redefining Problems

Objectives

Learn to ask key questions

Props

Writing materials

Activity Description

Sometimes problems are easier to solve if children restate or broaden the problem. There are two key questions that help children do this. These are: What do I want to find out? And, What words can I change to help me understand the problem?

Actions
Preschool Warm-up
   Talk to your child about recent problems at home or at school and share in making a list of problems.

Preschool Workout
   After talking about a problem, help your child state the facts. Finally, help him rephrase the problem.
   Suppose your child said, "I want to ride the tricycle, and Susan won't let me." The parent-child dialogue might go like this.

   Parent: Tell me what happened.
   Child: Susan was riding and wouldn't get off. I told her to get off and she said no.
   Parent: What else happened?
   Child: I grabbed the handlebar, but the teacher made me let go.
   Parent: Now that you've explained it, let's say what the problem is again.

   Help your child restate the problem. Now talk about other problems your child is having, and try to redefine them.

Early and Later Elementary Warm-up
   Ask your child to write a list of problems bothering him. Share in making the list. This will give you an opportunity to discuss serious misunderstandings.

Early and Late Elementary Workout
   Choose the two most troublesome problems from the list, and write a sentence describing each problem.
   Say "What are the facts about this problem?"
   Say "What words can you change to make the problem clearer?"
   After your child has rewritten the problem, discuss it, and choose the best solution.

Preschool and Elementary Cool Down
   Gather your family to write and play an imagination game. If your child is a preschooler, you will need to write

the game, but ask your child for input. Many elementary age children will enjoy writing the game. A summary of the rules are:

1. One family member leads the game.

2. Players sit quietly, eyes closed, with their heads resting on their arms.

3. When the leader asks questions or gives directions, don't speak out.

4. Don't make the game too long. Adjust it to the age of your youngsters.

Notes

1. Terry McDaniels Masters, "The Critical Thinking Workout," *Instructor,* February 1991.

2. Donald Dinkmeyer and Gary McKay, *The Parents Handbook* (Circle Pines, Minn.: American Guidance Service, 1982), adapted from 97-102.

3. Kent Garland Burtt, *Smart Times* (New York: William Morrow and Co., 1984), 99.

4. Elaine Martin, *Baby Games* (Philadelphia: Running Press, 1988), 115.

5. Susan Amerikaner, *101 Things to Do to Develop Your Child's Gifts and Talents* (New York: Tom Doherty Associates, 1989).

6. McDaniels Masters, 64.

7. Sidney Parnes, "Idea Stimulating Techniques," *The Journal of Creative Behavior,* Second Quarter, 1976.

APPENDIX

Imagineering Games

Imagineering Game Script

The following game rules and outline will help you play and write your own family imagineering games. Feel free to follow the outline, to ignore it, or develop an outline of your own. Repeat the imagineering rules for the first game or two; after that your child will probably remember them. Here are some helpful rules for your family's imagineering, followed by seven imagineering games.

1. The leader gives the directions and reads the imagineering story.

2. Players sit in a comfortable position with their eyes closed.

3. Players nod yes or no instead of answering questions or speaking out loud while the game is in progress.

4. Listen carefully and try not to interrupt the leader.

Script Outline

Choose an imaginary incident._____
_____ .

Describe the central character.
    What does it look like? _____ .
    Can it change its shape, size, color, appearance (follow the Discovery Checklist)? _____ .
    What adventures will it have? _____ .
How does the script end? _____
_____ .
Additional activities? _____
_____ .

The Aquarium

Have you ever visited an aquarium? It's fun to go to an aquarium because it's a place where different kinds of sea animals live. There are fish of different sizes and colors. Some look weird.

Think of the strange sea creatures you've seen or read about. . . . Close your eyes and imagine one of them.

Picture in your mind the way it looks. . . . Now think of another sea creature. What does it look like? . . . Make it a different kind of creature.

Put the two together. What kind of a beast do they make? . . . What color is your new sea animal? . . . Give it a name that tells something about your creature.

Pretend that your sea creature can change its size by sucking in or blowing out air. . . . Can you hear it huff and puff? . . . Make it into an enormous creature. . . . How big is it? . . . Shrink it into a tiny creature.

Is it small enough to make it your pet sea monster? . . . What does it look like in a fish bowl? . . . Have you named it yet?

Oops. It's beginning to grow again. What now? . . . Fill the bathroom sink with water and put your pet creature in it. . . . It's still growing and doesn't fit in the sink.

Hurry, fill the bathtub with water and put the creature in it. . . . What does it look like now? . . . Is it friendly? . . . What did you say to the creature when you took it to the bathtub?

It's still growing and its head and tail are hanging out of the tub, dripping water on the floor. . . . You know it can't stay in the bathtub.

Put your creature in the back of the car and start looking for a swimming pool. . . . By the way, how did you carry it from the tub to the car? . . . Imagine what it looks like in a swimming pool.

Maybe if you ask your pet creature to stop growing it will, and you can take it back to the aquarium. . . . If you talk nicely to sea monsters, they usually do what you ask.

Is it small now? . . . I think I hear its air whooshing out. Can you hear it? . . . Wait a second until the creature is small again.

Put your creature back in the fish bowl and take it to the aquarium. . . . Tell your creature good-bye and slip it into the fish tank. . . . What did it say to you?

How would you feel if you saw the sea creature again? Draw a picture of your adventure.

The Circus

It's fun and exciting to go to a circus because there are funny clowns, trained animals, and men and women who perform dangerous acts. Think about the different acts in a circus. . . . What is your favorite act? . . . Imagine that you are performing it. . . . When you finish, take a bow for the crowd.

Pretend that you are one of the clowns. What kind of an act are your doing? . . . Picture it in your mind. . . . What costume are you wearing?

The clown who is the human cannonball is sick today. Since you are a clown, volunteer to be the human cannonball. How do you feel? . . . Are you scared?

Slide into the barrel of the cannon and feel the smooth sides with your hands. What's it like in there? . . .

Is it dark? . . . What happens to your voice? . . . What are you thinking now?

KaaaBooom. The cannon fires, and you're on your way. Feel the wind blow against your body as you blast toward the top of the circus tent. . . . Spread your arms and do a flip. . . . Is the crowd below getting smaller as you go up?

Something's wrong, because you're not coming down, you're floating higher and higher. You're flying! You fly right out the top of the circus tent and into the sky. Is the sky changing color as you fly higher? . . . Make the sky any color. . . . What does the sky look like?

Look down and find your home. It's getting smaller and smaller, and you know it is time to go back. There's a parachute strapped on your back. . . . Find the cord and give it a tug. . . . Imagine you are gently floating toward the circus tent. . . . Can you see your home? . . . How does it look now?

Drift slowly through the top of the circus tent and land gracefully in the center ring. Wave to the cheering crowd. It's nice to be on the ground again.

Act out your adventure and ask your family to be the audience.

The World's Strangest Automobile

Close your eyes and imagine your favorite automobile. It can be a real car or an imaginary one. Pick the style of car you like best.

Imagine what your car looks like. . . . Give it a name and add your favorite color. . . . Shine it up. . . . Now add as many colors as you like. . . . What does it look like now?

If you take a part away or add a new part some pretty funny things can happen. Let's try it on your automobile. Suppose you took away one or more of the wheels. What does it look like going down the street? . . . Arrange the remaining wheels so your car is balanced. . . . Have you ever seen a car with less than four wheels? . . . Does yours look like it?

Now imagine your car as an extra long limousine. How long is it? . . . Add some wheels. . . . Where will you put them? . . . Add all the wheels you want to make it a better car.

It's time to change your car again. Imagine that it can travel on railroad tracks and fly. Now what does it look like? . . . What do you need to add or take away to make this kind of car? . . . What does it look like now?

You're tired of riding in a big car, so invent the smallest car in the world. How will it be different from other cars? . . . Change it to your favorite color and add other colors you like. . . . Change the controls so kids can drive the car. . . . What does it look like now? Will your mom or dad fit in it? . . . Drive your new car to school and show it off. . . . What does your class think of the car you've invented?

Pretend it's a holiday. . . . Take your car for a drive. How will you travel? . . . By railroad track, by highway, by air, some other way? . . . Pretend that it will do anything you want it to do. . . . You can go anywhere you want to go. Where will you go?

The day's over, so drive your car home. Since it is an imaginary car, make it the right size to fit in the garage next to your parents' car. Go in the house and relax because you have worked hard inventing.

Cut and paste car pictures from magazines or newspapers to make different imaginary cars.

Boxes

Boxes are fun to play with because you can make different things with them. You can use your imagination to change the box to whatever you want. Lean back in your chair, close your eyes, and think about different kinds of boxes.

Pretend that you have a box about as big as a refrigerator. Imagine that you can change it to any size you want. Change it to a huge box, then a tiny box. Imagine that your mom told you to pick up your clothes and toys and put them away. It's a big job because you haven't done it for awhile, and they are all over the room.

Picture all the toys and clothes that need to be put away in the box. How big is the pile? . . . Is everything there? . . . Keep piling them on. . . . Now imagine that you can make a wish and it will happen. . . . Wish that the clothes and toys in the box are put away. . . . What happened? . . . What does the house look like now?

Let's try something else with your box. Imagine that it shrinks to a small box. Make it the right size for a pet. Any animal you want for a pet is OK. . . . Combine two or three animals and make an imaginary pet. . . . What does it look like? . . . Stop for a few minutes and draw a picture of your new pet.

Go back to the box. Change your box into two boxes, a huge one and a tiny one. Pretend that the big box is a space station, and the small one is a space shuttle. The space station is filled with people. What kind of clothes are they wearing? . . . Do they have on space suits? . . . What planets are they near?

Help the space shuttle come in for a landing. Where do the people live that are on the shuttle? . . . What do they look like?

Get another box, because it's time for your flight back to earth. For the return trip the box is only big enough for you and a friend. Imagine what your space ship looks like. . . . Can you walk around in this space ship? . . . De-

sign the inside of the ship so you will be comfortable. . . .
Do you have everything you need?

You are at the controls of the space ship, ready for blast-
off. . . . Check your controls . . . brace yourself. . . . you're
off! Fly around the space station once before you head
home. Look around so you will remember what space
looks like. Push the button that puts your ship on automatic control and stretch, . . . you will be home soon.

Would you like to make another space trip? Don't throw
away your big box. You might need it again.

When Moses Was a Baby

Read the Bible story of Moses in Exodus 2:1-10. His parents were in a tight spot, but God helped them think of a plan to save Moses' life.

Try to imagine what it was like to be in Egypt thousands of years ago. To make matters worse, you are the Israelite slave of Pharaoh's daughter, and you must obey or be punished. You are wading in the Nile River with Pharaoh's daughter when you see something floating in the reeds along the river bank. You are ordered to pull it in; it's a baby in a basket.

What does the baby look like? . . . How did you feel when you found the baby? . . . What did Pharaoh's daughter think when she looked at the baby Moses?

Do you think anyone told Pharaoh about Moses? Imagine what Pharaoh said. . . . Imagine what Moses thought about when he was ten years old.

Happy Birthday

A birthday is fun and exciting because it's your special day. Think of your best birthday. What were some of the presents you received? Do you remember the cake?

Imagine that your favorite birthday cake is in front of you. It's a special cake because each time you eat a piece, the cake returns to it original size.

Suppose you want to share the cake with your class at school. Make the cake large enough for everyone to have a big piece. How large is the cake? . . . Are all of your friends getting enough to eat?

You want to give a small cake to each of your friends. Ask the cake to divide into small cakes and see what will happen? . . . Let each kid choose his favorite kind of cake. Think of all the flavors the cake could be. . . . Do all of the kids have miniature cakes to take home?

There's one small cake left, but you feel stuffed. Who would you like to give the cake to? . . . Is there someone special? . . . Ask the cake to change its size. . . . Did it change to another flavor, too? . . . Make it the best flavor in the world. What does it taste like now? . . . Do you still want to eat it?

Your cake tastes so good that you decide to enter it in "The Best Cake in the World" contest. Think about what it looks like. . . . Describe it to yourself. . . . How yummy is it? . . . You can't stand it any longer, go ahead and take a bite. . . . Imagine the great taste of the cake.

The judges decide your cake is the best in the world. What is your prize? . . . You can take your cake home now. . . . Don't eat it all, because if you leave some, it will always grow into the cake you want.

Talk to your family about your cake. Did anyone else imagine one like it? . . . Ask if you can bake a cake and see what your mom says.

A Trip to Jerusalem

Do you wonder how Jesus looked and talked, and what His house looked like? There aren't any real pictures of Jesus, so we can't be sure about the color of His hair or eyes, how tall He was, or what His voice sounded like. Draw a picture of Jesus in your mind.

Pretend that you are in Jerusalem with your mom and dad. The streets are crowded, and people are busy. Your parents stop at some small markets to buy what they need.

Walk ahead of them and look for a toy you want to buy. Remember, no video games, trucks, or battery-operated toys; buy something that kids played with 2,000 years ago.

What do you want to buy? . . . How does it look? . . . Is it large, small, colored? . . . Is it for boys . . . for girls?

You're ahead of your parents. You look around for them, but instead you see a crowd of people, and you're curious about what's happening.

Run over to the crowd. . . . Some of the people in the crowd are talking to a man they call Jesus and Teacher. What are they talking about? . . . What are His friends doing?

He's looking right at you. . . . You don't know what to do. . . . Look at His face. . . . Think about how you feel.

Many boys and girls are sitting or standing around Jesus. There are little kids and big ones, too. Pretend that you are one of the little kids. . . . Jesus is motioning for you to come over to Him . . . Go ahead, don't be scared.

He picks you up and holds you. What does He say to you? . . . Go ahead, put your arms around Him and give Him a hug. Jesus is talking to the crowd about little kids. . . . What do you think He's saying?

There's your mom and dad. They look a little worried. Jesus smiles and puts you down. You know that it is time to leave. Tell Jesus good-bye and walk over to your mom and dad.

Think about Jesus and slowly open your eyes. You're home. Write a prayer thanking Jesus for loving you.